Samuel French Acting Edition

Boston Theater Marathon of Ten-Minute Plays

SAMUELFRENCH.COM   SAMUELFRENCH.CO.UK

Copyright © 2000 by Baker's Plays, Inc.
All Rights Reserved

BOSTON THEATER MARATHON OF TEN-MINUTE PLAYS is fully protected under the copyright laws of the United States of America, the British Commonwealth, including Canada, and all other countries of the Copyright Union. All rights, including professional and amateur stage productions, recitation, lecturing, public reading, motion picture, radio broadcasting, television and the rights of translation into foreign languages are strictly reserved.

ISBN 978-0-874-40134-9

www.SamuelFrench.com
www.SamuelFrench.co.uk

For Production Enquiries

United States and Canada
Info@SamuelFrench.com
1-866-598-8449

United Kingdom and Europe
Plays@SamuelFrench.co.uk
020-7255-4302

Each title is subject to availability from Samuel French, depending upon country of performance. Please be aware that *BOSTON THEATER MARATHON OF TEN-MINUTE PLAYS* may not be licensed by Samuel French in your territory. Professional and amateur producers should contact the nearest Samuel French office or licensing partner to verify availability.

CAUTION: Professional and amateur producers are hereby warned that *BOSTON THEATER MARATHON OF TEN-MINUTE PLAYS* is subject to a licensing fee. Publication of this play(s) does not imply availability for performance. Both amateurs and professionals considering a production are strongly advised to apply to Samuel French before starting rehearsals, advertising, or booking a theatre. A licensing fee must be paid whether the title(s) is presented for charity or gain and whether or not admission is charged. Professional/Stock licensing fees are quoted upon application to Samuel French.

No one shall make any changes in this title(s) for the purpose of production. No part of this book may be reproduced, stored in a retrieval system, or transmitted in any form, by any means, now known or yet to be invented, including mechanical, electronic, photocopying, recording, videotaping, or otherwise, without the prior written permission of the publisher. No one shall upload this title(s), or part of this title(s), to any social media websites.

For all enquiries regarding motion picture, television, and other media rights, please contact Samuel French.

MUSIC USE NOTE

Licensees are solely responsible for obtaining formal written permission from copyright owners to use copyrighted music in the performance of this play and are strongly cautioned to do so. If no such permission is obtained by the licensee, then the licensee must use only original music that the licensee owns and controls. Licensees are solely responsible and liable for all music clearances and shall indemnify the copyright owners of the play(s) and their licensing agent, Samuel French, against any costs, expenses, losses and liabilities arising from the use of music by licensees. Please contact the appropriate music licensing authority in your territory for the rights to any incidental music.

IMPORTANT BILLING AND CREDIT REQUIREMENTS

If you have obtained performance rights to this title, please refer to your licensing agreement for important billing and credit requirements.

TABLE OF CONTENTS

Forward	6
GRASSY KNOLL	7
THE TWELVE FORTY	17
POKER FACE	27
MANAGED CARE	35
TESTIMONY	45
THE YELLOW BUS	55
TAKING ROOT	63
FLAG GIRLS	75
MIRROR MAN	85
DOWN	97
FRANCE	107
THE LESSON	115
SHOTGUN WEDDING	121
ORAL REPORT	125
PEAS	135
VIRGIN TERRITORY	141
LATE ARRIVAL	151
BENITA'S CHOICE: HAROLD'S SAY	159
MEN ARE FROM MILWAUKEE, WOMEN ARE FROM PHOENIX	167
DUET FOR SHY PEOPLE	175
QUE SERA, SERA	197
CHANCE OF YOUR LIFE	207
FANTASIA FAIR	217
ROOM 69	229
Playwright Biographies	241

BOSTON THEATER MARATHON
OF TEN-MINUTE PLAYS

Foreword

At 12:00 noon on Sunday, April 18, 1999, forty theatres in the Boston area came together at Boston Playwrights' Theatre to perform one ten-minute play each. It took stamina; it took imagination; and it took guts from everyone involved: the playwrights, the theatres, the actors, the directors, the technicians, and most of all, from the audiences. From noon until closing—9:59pm sharp—the performers played to standing-room-only crowds, some of whom had spent the last ten hours rooted to their seats by the exciting, funny, tragic, absurd, surprising wealth of new works for the stage. By the end of the evening, we had established a Boston tradition. We did it again on Sunday, April 16, 2000, and the crowds came back for more. The Boston Theatre Critics Association gave us a special citation "for enlivening local theater through the annual showcase of short plays at Boston Playwrights' Theatre," and, in two years, we made over $20,000 for two worthy non-profit organizations: the Boston Theatre Benevolent Fund and the Children's AIDS Program at the Boston Medical Center.

But the best news is that the Boston Theater Marathon continues to pull brand new audiences into the theatre. The experience is very like the famous Boston Marathon itself—it's fast, it's furious, it's dramatic, it's funny, and it's over before you know it. It's better than tv, and there are no commercials!

So... read on! The plays in this wonderful anthology have a flavor of the first day we ran the marathon—they're exciting, witty, surprising, and infinitely entertaining. Enjoy!

— Kate Snodgrass
Artistic Director
Boston Theater Marathon

GRASSY KNOLL

by

Barbara Blatner

THE BOSTON THEATER MARATHON

Grassy Knoll was first produced in New York in Turnip Theatre's 1997 Fifteen-minute Play Festival. It was directed by Nicole Potter with the following cast:
STACE .... Natalie Cook
DAVID .... Thomas Gamburg

Grassy Knoll was produced at the First Annual Boston Theater Marathon on April 18th, 1999, sponsored by The Emerson Stage and directed by Steven Yakutis. The cast was as follows:
DAVID .... Richard B. Caines
STACE .... Sarah Jane O'Donnell

> *This play is dedicated to those of us*
> *who remember where we were at*
> *the moment of Kennedy's assassination.*

CHARACTERS

STACE — 17, white, a high school senior
DAVID — 17, black, a high school senior, at a different school than Stace

SETTING

Dallas, November 22, 1963. The grassy knoll overlooking the route of John Kennedy's motorcade.

NOTE: The play can be performed with a companion piece, *Years of Sky*, or by itself.

GRASSY KNOLL

(*Stace and David sit together on the grassy knoll, waiting, with other spectators, for Kennedy's approach. David is tickling Stace vigorously.*)

STACE. (*Laughing.*) Stop! Will you please stop it! I'm gonna wet my pants! (*He gets a ticklish spot.*) Nooo! Stop it, I can't stand — there! David! (*She fends him off. He keeps grabbing at her.*) You always do that to me! I shouldn't have told you where my secret spots are. (*Beat: he's grinning.*) Oh you're very glad I did, aren't you, you little beast! (*Beat: he feints at her. Now she grabs him, to tickle him, he pushes her away, rolls over on his back. She gives up, sticks out her tongue at him. Beat.*) I'm mad at you, David!

DAVID. (*Beat: he grins at her.*) You were with your fancy friends.

STACE. Why'd you disappear like that?

DAVID. (*Beat: he grins at her, he's testing her.*) I didn't think — you didn't need me, did you?

STACE. I was really upset! I couldn't believe you just walked out! I looked all over for you!

DAVID. (*Beat.*) Really? (*Pause: they look at each other. Stace is exasperated.*)

STACE. I'm going to get a soda. (*She starts to go, he*

pulls her back.)

DAVID. Can't you wait? I don't want you to miss anything.

STACE. It'll take two minutes — (*She's slapping at him, half playful, half angry.*)

DAVID. (*Over Stace's line:*) He'll be here any minute. (*Beat.*)

STACE. I gotta go back for soccer practice at four.

DAVID. Why don't you take practice off? I don't get to see you on school days.

STACE. We lucked out today, didn't we? I get to see you *and* the beautiful President. (*Pause: he's trying to read her — they grin at each other. Stace points to the street; David looks.*)

DAVID. No. It's a hearse. It moves at the same pace as the motorcade. Joey has a friend who drives a hearse. Think that's morbid?

STACE. (*Beat.*) Not really. It's kinda — I dunno — flashy. Fishy. Flashy-fishy, I dunno. (*Beat.*)

DAVID. Look at all the stupid policemen. See the guy behind me? He's secret service.

STACE. (*Turning around.*) How do you know?

DAVID. Don't look now! (*He grabs her, they giggle. Pause.*)

DAVID. This'll be the first moment I see him in person.

STACE. I wonder if he looks like his pictures. They're all fake, aren't they? (*David looks at her quizzically.*) My mother said they touch 'em up. (*In response, David slowly takes out a photo from a wallet in his pocket, shows it to her, looks for her reaction.*)

David. This is exactly what he looks like.

STACE. I didn't know you had a picture of him — how long have you had it-

DAVID. (*Interrupting.*) A year, maybe.

STACE. That was before you met me.

DAVID. Yeah.

STACE. (*Giggling.*) You mean you were actually alive before you met me?

DAVID. (*Beat: grinning at her.*) No. (*Pause: he looks at the photo.*) Nobody in my family voted for him.

STACE. My mother says the only reason she likes him is 'cause he's handsome. Think he's handsome?

DAVID. He's a lot more than handsome —

STACE. Oh yes. (*This is obviously something David has said before.*) He's passionate. He's beautiful.

DAVID. He is.

STACE. He's rich, you know.

DAVID. (*Beat.*) But he doesn't show it. Can I see you tonight?

STACE. Well I hope so. We planned on it, didn't we? (*Pause: he strokes her hair.*) Did you tell anyone you were kicking the school habit this afternoon? (*He shakes his head.*) We'd never get away with that at our school. Anyone who wanted to come had to get a note from their mother.

DAVID. Your school's much fancier than mine.

STACE. (*She sticks out her tongue at him.*) Your school's more fun than mine.

DAVID. Oh right. (*Beat.*) Hey, you know Dreadhead, I told you about him? We're now trying to raise his level of dread as much as we can? (*Beat: he has her attention.*) We took his history book this morning and glued pages from a magazine in it.

STACE. What magazine?

DAVID. Playboy.

STACE. Ohhh. You are not so shy! (*David looks*

away. She tickles him a little.)

DAVID. He tried to pretend nothing was wrong. He picked up the book at the beginning of class, opened it up, and put it back down. He showed not one sign in his eyes at all.

STACE. You weirdos.

DAVID. He's really boring. He is boring. It's like a crime. (*She laughs.*) What should we do —

STACE. (*Over his line, tense, playing with her hair.*) What —

DAVID. — tonight? What should we do?

STACE. (*Beat.*) Did you sleep with Janey Potter? (*Suddenly aware of people around her, she gestures "oops," putting her hand over her mouth.*) David — did you — ? (*Pause: David doesn't answer.*)

STACE. Did you? (*David just smiles an ambiguous smile.*) You're not gonna tell me, are you? You always do this. I can't find out either, can I, she goes to your school. It's like you're in a different world. (*Pause, David continues smiling at her. She slaps him. Then he looks again at the photo.*)

DAVID. You know what? I'm gonna try to meet him today. I'm gonna find out where they're having their big meeting. I want to shake his hand. (*Beat: he holds up the photo, squints at it.*) I see a lot in his eyes, you know. It's like, if he met you, he would actually — look at you. All he would have to do is look at you, and he would know who you are. Who I am. (*He puts the picture back in his wallet.*) Most people's eyes are boring.

STACE. You and your boredom.

DAVID. (*Beat.*) You know me, don't you.

STACE. I see into the hidden recesses of your brain. (*She teasingly bores her forefinger into his forehead.*)

Bbbzzz. I see your cranial mountains! (*He stands, and pulls her to her feet, to look at the street.*)

DAVID. But you can't see everything, can you?

STACE. (*Earnest.*) You think I care if you did it with her but I don't.

DAVID. You don't?

STACE. I'm just interested to see what *your* life is like.

DAVID. Really? (*She nods.*) Well what's your life like?

STACE. (*Pointing to the street.*) It's coming! (*David holds Stace from behind, doesn't look at the street.*)

DAVID. Tell me what you see.

STACE. Don't you wanna look — (*He shakes his head.*) Black cars. Moving real slow. All these little flags blowing around.

DAVID. See anybody yet?

STACE. No. (*Beat.*) David? my parents are going away for the weekend. Actually — they're going tonight.

DAVID. (*Disappointed.*) So you have to babysit Lucy and Teddy-

STACE. (*Over his line.*) They're taking them. They decided last night.

DAVID. You're alone there tonight?

STACE. (*Beat: they look at each other.*) Yep. Look at all these people!

DAVID. When are they —

STACE. Oh they'll be long gone by the time I get home. They're visiting my grandmother. Did I tell you that? (*Beat: he looks at her.*) The sun's huge, isn't it? (*Beat.*) The sky — it's empty — it's like — blank. Just think: everyone here came to look at this one person.

DAVID. So — should I come over tonight? (*Beat: they look at each other.*)

STACE. (*Mock terror, excitement.*) Aaaaaaaa!
DAVID. (*Laughing.*) What —
STACE. (*Laughing.*) What —
DAVID. I have to help Dad and Joey early tomorrow —
STACE. I'd really want you to stay over —
DAVID. Where would we —
STACE. My room... Maybe the room in the garage...
DAVID. I'll bring my records — I could bring a whole stack —
STACE. But we'll only play a few, right, right? I mean — know what I mean? (*He has a brief coughing fit. She nuzzles him; he tickles her a little.*) You can't tickle me tonight. I'm making rules already. (*She's behind him, not looking at the street.*) Do you see him yet? (*David shakes his head.*) Tell me what you see.
DAVID. Black cars. Moving very slow. (*Beat.*)
STACE. So — um — what time?
DAVID. What–
STACE. What? You know —
DAVID. (*Grinning at her.*) I do?
STACE. The time, sweet prince.
DAVID. I see him! She's next to him. She's got some pink dress on. The Governor's in the front? I can — can I come right after my father goes to work?
STACE. Yes! Yes yes yes!
DAVID. He looks just like his picture. I told you. (*David glances back at the "Secret Service" agent.*) Don't look, but you should see the guy. He's been looking at us this whole time now, his eyes're all over the place. (*They glance back, giggle.*)
STACE. We just read this huge book, Ulysses, and at the end this woman says, like, something like: yes yes yes I — put my arms around him and he could feel my —

perfumed breasts and I said yes I said yes yes yes! That's the last line! Of the book! (*David is laughing, and beaming at her.*) What? What?

DAVID. You'll be an actress.

STACE. Really? You know I wanna be. But it could be awful, too, don't you think, being an actress? You'd have to be so involved in the world. The world is dangerous. The world is treacherous. Would you want that — after we're —

DAVID. (*Beat: he looks at her.*) Eight-thirty. Eight.

STACE. Yes. Yes yes yes! Look at her hat!

DAVID. Will it be weird in your parent's house?

STACE. Everything's weird.

DAVID. (*Beat; then, imitating someone.*) Weird, huh?

STACE. (*Delight.*) That's just the way they do it!

DAVID. (*Encouraged by her response.*) Weird, man, huh? Very weird. Very very weird, very morbid, man, huh? (*She shakes her head. Pause: she watches the street, he still isn't looking, is perhaps playing with her hair.*)

STACE. This is the longest day! I'm so nervous!

DAVID. I think — this is the most important day of my life.

STACE. Are you nervous?

DAVID. (*Beat; then, pretending.*) Nah. (*Beat, then simply:*) I'm going to get caught in your arms forever. (*They hug passionately, kiss briefly, then he holds her so that he's looking at the street and she's not.*)

DAVID. Look! Don't you wanna see? It's him, Stace. Don't you wanna see?! (*She shakes her head, holds onto him, plays with his hair; he holds her tighter, watches the street. The crowd starts to clap. With his arms still around her, he claps.*)

* * *

THE TWELVE FORTY

by

Barry Brodsky

18   THE BOSTON THEATER MARATHON

The Twelve Forty was performed at the First Annual Boston Theater Marathon on April 18th, 1999. Sponsored by Playwrights' Platform. Directed by Thomas Grimes. The cast was as follows:

BLACK .... Michael Nurse
WHITE .... John Carozza

for Nan

CHARACTERS

WHITE MAN
BLACK MAN

TIME
NOW

PLACE
AMERICA

THE TWELVE FORTY

(*An outdoor railroad station platform on a chilly evening. There should be a bench or two chairs upstage. A White Man in his mid-to-late 20's is standing waiting for a train. He is fairly well dressed in a suit and overcoat; perhaps a young stockbroker or banker. He seems impatient. Enter a poorly dressed young Black Man with an unlit cigarette in his mouth. The White Man glances at the Black Man and then quickly looks at his watch. The Black Man nods to him but he doesn't return the nod. As the Black Man slowly approaches him, the White Man nervously look at his watch again. He turns slightly so that he isn't facing the Black Man. Finally, as the Black Man sidles up next to him, the White Man looks at his watch once more, and awaits what he is certain will be a request for money or worse.*)

BLACK. Got a match?

WHITE. I don't smoke.

BLACK. That make you live forever? (*Puts cigarette in pocket.*) You got the time?

WHITE. No.

BLACK. C'mon man, I just saw you lookin' at your watch. What time is it?

WHITE. (*Looks at watch.*) Twelve-ten.

BLACK. Twelve-ten?
WHITE. Yes.
BLACK. (*Beat.*) Nice watch you got there. (*Beat.*) Cost a pretty penny? (*Beat.*) I say, the watch. Cost a lot?
WHITE. Yes, yes, I suppose. (*Looks around.*)
BLACK. Nobody gonna be around here for another twenty, twenty-five minutes. Next train's at twelve-forty. Last one of the night. People start comin' round about twelve-thirty, twelve thirty-five. See I know when people come and when they go 'round here. I also know when folks start comin' up to get the train. So what do you figure, two, three thousand?
WHITE. Beg your pardon?
BLACK. Your watch. Two or three thousand?
WHITE. It's none of your...
BLACK. I'm just guessing of course. Four thousand?
WHITE. It, uh, was a gift.
BLACK. From your girlfriend? (*No response.*) Wife?
WHITE. It was from my mother.
BLACK. Your mother rich?
WHITE. My mother is dead.
BLACK. Mm. That's a shame. But you think she probably paid three or four thousand for it?
WHITE. Look, uh...
BLACK. You gotta admit, it's a real mind blower ain't it? Wearin' a four thousand dollar watch?
WHITE. I didn't say it...
BLACK. My own Mama? She used to tell that her father bought himself a house once for four thousand dollars. Four thousand dollars for a whole house. She told me that story a hundred times. Can you deal with that? Same price for a house as that there watch.
WHITE. I don't know if...

THE TWELVE FORTY 21

BLACK. My brother bought a new car once. When he was in the service. He fought in the war my oldest brother. Anyone in your family fight in that Vietnam War?

WHITE. No, I uh...

BLACK. Well he said the car dealers could get the monthly payments directly from Uncle Sam. Come right outta his check. Bought himself a brand new car for twenty-four hundred dollars. Nice car too.

WHITE. You want my watch? Is that what you want? My watch?

BLACK. Your watch?

WHITE. I told you my mother gave it to me goddam you.

BLACK. Hey buddy...

WHITE. (*Pulls gun out of overcoat.*) You want my watch?

BLACK. (*Steps back.*) Whoa there fella.

WHITE. You want my watch?

BLACK. I can't afford your watch, man.

WHITE. I'll give you something else instead.

BLACK. I don't want nothin' from you.

WHITE. Thought I was an easy target didn't you?

BLACK. I don't...

WHITE. Easy "rip off" as they say, right?

BLACK. You're crazy!

WHITE. Don't take another step.

BLACK. Look, look..

WHITE. Keep your hands up.

BLACK. They're up, they're up.

WHITE. You got a watch?

BLACK. What?

WHITE. You heard me, you got a watch?

BLACK. Why would I ask you what time it is if I had a

watch on.

WHITE. You got any money?

BLACK. What? Well, I, I don't know. I got a few bucks I guess.

WHITE. Let's have it.

BLACK. Oh come on man, what's wrong with you?

WHITE. You people don't like it when the tables get turned do you.

BLACK. What are you talking about?

WHITE. What have you got? Knife? Gun?

BLACK. You're the one with the gun man.

WHITE. Asking me all those questions about how I got my watch.

BLACK. I was making conversation. We got a long wait for the train.

WHITE. You weren't up here for no train.

BLACK. What else would I be doin' up here on a railroad platform?

WHITE. I don't look the type to carry a gun do I?

BLACK. Look pal, you got me all wrong. (*Brings hands down.*) I wasn't gonna do nothin' to you.

WHITE. Keep 'em up.

BLACK. (*Raises hands.*) Look, I live over there. In that building right behind you. The damned train goes past my window every night. Can't help knowin' what time it comes. I'm on my way to my sister's house. She just called me. Her boy's sick and I'm goin' over there to help her out. That's all there is to it. Honest.

WHITE. Take off your pants.

BLACK. Say what??

WHITE. I said take off your pants.

BLACK. You gotta be kiddin me. There's gonna be some people here soon.

THE TWELVE FORTY 23

WHITE. You do what I say, Boy.

BLACK. Now listen here...

WHITE. No, you listen here. I said take off your pants! I mean it. You know this isn't even a registered gun. I'll say it was yours and we struggled and it went off. They'll believe me. I'm a respectable citizen. You probably have a record a mile long.

BLACK. You got me confused with someone else man. I ain't never been in trouble. You don't know me.

WHITE. Your pants! Let's move it! (*Black Man slowly undoes his belt.*)

BLACK. What are you doin' up here anyway?

WHITE. C'mon get 'em off.

BLACK. Get your jollies shootin at black folks.

WHITE. C'mon take the pants off. The shoes. Everything.

BLACK. You crazy son of a bitch. It's cold out here.

WHITE. Strip! (*The Black Man slowly takes off all his clothes, mumbling "crazy bastard" etc, and piles them in front of him. He stands in just his underwear and socks, shivering.*) Now move back.

BLACK. (*Black Man backs up a few steps as the White Man starts to go through his clothes. He is looking through the pockets, etc., keeping an eye on the Black Man and an eye on the clothing. He puts the Black Man's wallet in his pocket and kicks the pile of clothes.*) Can I have my clothes back please?

WHITE. You want them back?

BLACK. Yes, please.

WHITE. Sure, here they are.

(*White Man takes the clothes and throws them off the platform down to the street below. As he does this, the Black Man screams and leaps at him. The White Man is caught off balance and the gun is jarred loose. The Black Man scrambles for the gun, grabs it off the ground, and comes up with it. White Man is backing up.)*

Don't shoot..
 BLACK. C'mon asshole. You know what to do.
 WHITE. I wasn't going to shoot you.
 BLACK. I said c'mon! Quick!
 WHITE. I never would have... Oh... Right. Alright. Just don't shoot. (*White Man slowly undresses.*)
 BLACK. C'mon, now you move it. And take off that watch too while you're at it. (*As the White Man throws down his pants, shirt, etc., the Black Man puts them on while keeping the White Man covered. The two men are wearing the exact same type/style of underwear.*)
 WHITE. Be careful. That suit's expensive... (*Finally, the White Man is nude except for his watch, underwear, shoes and stockings.*)
 BLACK. I said the watch.
 WHITE. It really was a gift from my mother.
 BLACK. My heart's breaking. C'mon. (*The White Man tosses the watch to the Black Man who catches it, studies it for a moment, then flings it off the platform.*)
 WHITE. Wha!! What'd you do that for??
 BLACK. I don't want nothin' of yours. You understand that? Nothin.
 WHITE. You're wearing my clothes! You have my gun!
 BLACK. Your gun? (*He flings the gun off the platform.*)
 WHITE. My gun! My watch!

BLACK. And as soon as I get home, I'm burning these here clothes.

WHITE. I, I'll freeze up here alone.

BLACK. There'll be some people comin up here in a few minutes. Maybe you can get one to call the cops for you.

WHITE. I, I just wanted to protect myself.

BLACK. I wasn't gonna do anything to you. I was foolin' with you a little. But I wasn't gonna do anything.

WHITE. I was afraid. (*The Black Man starts to leave but then stops and looks at the White Man standing on the platform shivering. He pauses for a moment.*)

BLACK. Ah what the hell... (*Black Man takes off the overcoat and throws it down in front of the White Man who picks it up and quickly puts it on.*)

WHITE. Thank you.

BLACK. No sense in you freezing to death. (*Black Man sits down, uncomfortably tries to adjust his new clothes, and looks down the track.*)

WHITE. (*Slowly approaching him.*) Are you... are you going to wait for the train?

BLACK. I'm not gonna miss the last train 'cause of you. 'Course my sister's gonna wonder where the hell I came up with clothes like these. (*White Man sits next to Black Man and joins him in looking down the track.*)

BLACK. Wonder what time it is.

WHITE. I wouldn't know. (*Both men look at each other, then look away for the train.*)

* * *

POKER FACE

by

Robert Brustein

28   THE BOSTON THEATER MARATHON

Poker Face premiered at the First Annual Boston Theater Marathon on April 18th, 1999. Sponsored by American Repertory Theatre. Directed by Bob McGrath. The cast was as follows:

BUSTER .... Alvin Epstein
ALAN .... Ben Evett

Dedicated to the spirit of Samuel Beckett

CHARACTERS

BUSTER KEATON — in his seventies, a former silent movie actor

ALAN SCHNEIDER — in his forties, a theatre director

TIME
The nineteen seventies.

PLACE
Keaton's shabby-genteel house in East L.A.

POKER FACE

(The living room of Buster Keaton's shabby genteel mansion in East Los Angeles. Memorabilia of his silent film days strewn about this unusually sloppy room. Stills of Buster in his various film triumphs, including The Navigator, The General, and Limelight with Charlie Chaplin. At rise, Buster, now over seventy, is alone sitting at a poker table, wearing shirt sleeves and suspenders, drinking a beer, examining his hand. He then rises to examine, one by one, the other hands on the table.)

BUSTER. Don't raise with two pair, dummy. Wait for the full house. *(The next hand.)* Draw for the flush. *(And the next.)* Fold. You got to know when to fold. When will you guys learn to play five card stud? *(A bell rings. And rings. Buster looks up, puzzled, then calls:)* Lionel! Lionel! *(No answer.)* LIONEL!! *(Pause, as he tries to remember.)* I guess it's Sunday, goddammit.

(Buster leaves the stage. The sound of a door opening. He then enters with a man in his early forties, wearing a suit and a baseball cap.)

Sorry. *(Very English.)* My man is off today. What did you say your name was?

ALAN. Schneider. Alan Schneider.

BUSTER. Well, take a seat, why don't you. (*Buster fixes himself another beer without offering one to Alan.*).

ALAN. (*After a strained pause.*) I'm really thrilled to meet you Mr. Keaton. I've been a fan of yours since I was a kid.

BUSTER. That's nice. Not many people remember Buster Keaton any more.

ALAN. Everybody remembers Buster Keaton. You were the funniest man in silents.

BUSTER. (*Looking at the poker hands.*) You must be thinking of the tramp. Me they called the saddest man in silents. (*Another pause.*)

ALAN. (*Looking at the table.*) You're in the middle of a poker game?

BUSTER. I've been in the middle of this poker game since 1927.

ALAN. (*Looking around.*) Where are the other players?

BUSTER. Dead.

ALAN. Dead?

BUSTER. This is Irving Thalberg's hand. This is Nicholas Schenk's. And this one here belongs to Eric Campbell. He was the heavy at Essenay. The tramp's company.

ALAN. The tramp?

BUSTER. You know. Chaplin. The little guy.

ALAN. (*Gravely.*) Oh.

BUSTER. They're all dead. (*Pause.*) Excepting me. The real sucker of the group is Thalberg. Always raises on two pair, the dummy. Owes me more than two million. (*Looks at Thalberg's hand again.*)

ALAN. So you always win?

BUSTER. Yeah.
ALAN. What's your secret.
BUSTER. My poker face.
ALAN. I see.
BUSTER. What's your game?
ALAN. Bridge.
BUSTER. No, I mean what's your game. What do you do for a living?
ALAN. I'm a theatre director.
BUSTER. Oh, you're that New York guy. I thought you were some sort of baseball player with that cap you're wearing.
ALAN. I always wear a baseball cap. It's my trademark. Like your poker face. (*Pause.*) Did you get a chance to read the script I sent you?
BUSTER. (*Going to a table to pick it up.*) You mean this piece of crap? Yeah.
ALAN. You didn't like it?
BUSTER. Couldn't understand a word. What is this thing? Doesn't even have a title.
ALAN. There's the title. Film.
BUSTER. Yeah, I know. Film. The fancy word they call the movies nowadays. But what's the name of this so-called film?
ALAN. There's the name. Film. Sam likes simple titles. He once wrote a play called Play.
BUSTER. Sam?
ALAN. Samuel Beckett. You never heard of him? (*Keaton nods "no".*) I sent you a comedy of his once. Waiting for Godot? About two tramps in the middle of nowhere? Bert Lahr ending up playing your part. The one you turned down.
BUSTER. Oh yeah, Godot. (*He pronounces it*

"Godette".) I remember something now. I didn't understand a word of that one either.

ALAN. I'm sorry. *(Pause.)* What about this... uh... movie? I hope you're not saying that part doesn't interest you, either.

BUSTER. Of course I'm interested. I'm no dummy. I don't turn down five thousand dollars for a three day shoot. That's the fee, right? Five thousand?

ALAN. That's right.

BUSTER. Then I'm in.

ALAN. Great!

BUSTER. But the script needs fixing.

ALAN. Fixing?

BUSTER. It don't make no sense. And I wouldn't say it's a whole bunch of laughs either. The show needs some goosing up. Maybe, my walk. *(He demonstrates.)*

ALAN. *(Doubtful.)* Sam... uh, I mean Mr. Beckett likes his actors to stick pretty close to the script.

BUSTER. *(Not hearing.)* One thing. You're going to have to cut out that bit with the cat. Dogs I can work with, especially chihuahuas. Chihuahua are good actors. But not cats. Never get on stage with kids or cats.

ALAN. I'll mention it to Mr. Beckett.

BUSTER. I could do that bit where I sharpen my pencil and it gets smaller and smaller. Sure fire.

ALAN. We don't normally pad Samuel Beckett material.

BUSTER. Because you can tell your Mr. Beckett that his movie is too short. It won't last four minutes. Even if we stretched out the cat and dog business. *(Confidentially.)* For a percentage of the gross I could give him some ideas about how to make it longer.

ALAN. Mr. Beckett doesn't usually accept co-authors.

KEATON. (*Not hearing.*) And tell him I've got to wear one of my hats. What do you think of this Stetson? (*Puts it on.*)

ALAN. I can't imagine you doing a film without one of your hats.

BUSTER. Right. I got twelve of them, all different colors.

ALAN. I'll check it out with Mr. Beckett.

BUSTER. Check out one more thing. The lighting. I don't want any of those newfangled lighting effects. People got to see my face.

ALAN. Of course.

BUSTER. It's been my livelihood all these years.

ALAN. Of course.

BUSTER. (*Relaxing a little.*) In the old days, in the Keaton studios, we never used a script. Just started with a character in trouble, then improvised and lollygagged until we figured out how to get him out of his fix.

ALAN. I'm sure Mr. Beckett would be very interested in any business you can bring to his film.

BUSTER. Okay, it's a deal. Tell your Mr. Beckett I'll do this Shakespeare stuff of his. Tell your Mr. Beckett Buster Keaton is in. I guess.

ALAN. He'll be very happy. (*He stands up to shake Buster's hand.*) I am, too.(*He takes his coat.*) We start shooting in New York in six weeks. (*Holds out his hand. Keaton ignores it.*) It's been a real pleasure, Mr. Keaton. (*He exits.*)

BUSTER. (*Uncaps another beer, and goes back to the poker table. Hovering in turn over each player's hand.*) (*To Thalberg's.*) You missed the full boat again, Irving. (*To Schencks's.*) I wouldn't bluff on that load of crap, you dummy. (*To Campbell's.*) You were right to fold.

(Triumphantly, revealing his own hand.) Four ladies.
(Buster rakes in the chips as the lights fade.)

* * *

MANAGED CARE

by

Bill Cunningham

Managed Care premiered at the First Annual Boston Theater Marathon on April 18th, 1999. Sponsored by Mad Horse Theatre Company. Directed by Andrew Sokoloff. The cast was as follows:

GOODSELL .... Guy Durichek
TIZZY .... Kymberly Dakin

To Luke, Jenna, and Sam.

CHARACTERS

JAMES NELSON GOODSELL — A thirtysomething, corporate father figure.
TIZZY TYLER-GOODSELL — The thirtysomething, ex-wife of James Nelson Goodsell.

TIME
Present

PLACE
A corporate office

MANAGED CARE

(*A corporate office. James Nelson Goodsell is talking on a cellular phone.*)

GOODSELL. (*To the phone.*) Upgrade, Bernie. You need to upgrade. Your old system is crapola. It's no longer ... What's the word? What's the word I'm looking for?

(*Tizzy Tyler-Goodsell, who sits in an overstuffed, leather chair, reading the inside cover to a board game, says, without looking up...*)

TIZZY. Viable.
GOODSELL. You're no longer viable, Bernie. People today want to browse... surf... link. They want to feel connected at the click of a finger. E mail... chat rooms... Pornography. A miracle, Bernie. World wide access in the privacy of your own home. It's a modern miracle. (*Grabbing a handful of M&M's out of a bowl.*)
TIZZY. (*Reading from the board game cover.*) "The object of the game is to feed the world."
GOODSELL. (*Switching ears.*) Don't be ridiculous. Everybody believes in miracles. (*Popping an M&M into his mouth.*)
TIZZY. (*Reading.*) "The youngsters role play food-rich nations who gather apples, plums, pears and cherries before

the hungry raven eats them all."
GOODSELL. We can't afford to become personally involved. We're in the insurance business.
TIZZY. Premium.
GOODSELL. We care at a premium.
TIZZY. Stock and trade.
GOODSELL. That's our stock and trade. Reality number one.
TIZZY. Which leads to reality number two.
GOODSELL. Happiness... Happiness, Bernie! We insure it. We write policies that allow people to be personally irresponsible. Reckless. Secure in the knowledge that their beneficiaries will be better off without them.
TIZZY. God forbid.
GOODSELL. God forbid. (*Popping an M&M.*)
TIZZY. (*Reading.*) "Wearing culturally authentic clothing from their dress-up boxes - sold separately - the children take their baskets full of juicy, non-toxic fruits and distribute them evenly to the poor."
GOODSELL. I'm aware of stock prices! What, you think I need you to remind me of stock prices? I have the Wall Street Journal to remind me of stock prices!
TIZZY. "Some of the children — the sympathetic bird lovers in the group — will even leave a little something for our fine-feathered friend."
GOODSELL. (*Switching ears.*) I don't need you to tell me about initial offerings! Prices fluctuate! Worth isn't a constant! Everything is artificially inflated! Everything! Everything from a stock price to the importance of any one man to a company! (*Tizzy takes a non-toxic wooden apple and a non-toxic wooden pear out of the game box.*)
GOODSELL. Threatening! Who's threatening? I'm just

MANAGED CARE 39

talking realities. (*Tizzy knocks the wooden apple against the wooden pear. Knock. Knock.*)

GOODSELL. (*Switching ears again.*) Once-upon-a-time, Bernie, we sold term, variable and whole. We traded in a value stock. But now we're in a market economy and we need to turn value into growth. And that means we can't afford to be thinking about term life and variable life and whole life. We have to be thinking about shelf life. (*Popping an M&M.*) It's an adjustment. (*Popping another M&M.*) We're not answerable to individual policy holders anymore. We're answerable to the Market and — God knows — the Market doesn't give a rat's ass about health and well being.

TIZZY. Reality number three.

GOODSELL. Mutual Funds. People expect a healthy return on their investment.

TIZZY. Bottom line. Give him the bottom line.

GOODSELL. We no longer sell term, variable, or whole. We sell Limited Life... The prudent-man rule no longer applies... Bernie...? You there...? Bernie? (*Goodsell lowers the phone.*)

TIZZY. What happened?

GOODSELL. He quit.

TIZZY. Who?

GOODSELL. Bernie.

TIZZY. Bernie quit?

GOODSELL. Just like that.

TIZZY. But he was like a father to us.

GOODSELL. Never would have pegged it.

TIZZY. He gave us our first jobs as policy writers. Remember?

GOODSELL. A quitter.

TIZZY. He afforded us such a nice life.

GOODSELL. He didn't afford us this, Tizzy. We earned this. We were entitled to this. Every trapping.

TIZZY. Self-made?

GOODSELL. That's all I'm saying. (*Returning the phone to it's holder.*) Big baby... No one likes a quitter ... Isn't that what we're teaching the boy? That "winners never quit and quitters never prosper?"

TIZZY. Still... we may owe him a little something.

GOODSELL. Gratitude?

TIZZY. That's all I'm saying.

GOODSELL. Gratitude enslaves people. It makes them emotionally hamstrung. I choose not to be indebted to loyalty. Indebtedness leads to subordination and subordination leads to...

TIZZY. Submission?

GOODSELL. Emotional blackmail.

TIZZY. Like marriage.

GOODSELL. The worst submission of all. "I" becomes "us" to the point where there's no "you" there's only "we." A hostile-take-over of the heart. An unhealthy merger. Bad policy. We were smart to divest when we did. Who knows what might have come of it. The important thing is we've been able to make divorce work. (*Popping an M&M.*) We have a healthy respect for each other's individuality.

TIZZY. Still...

GOODSELL. The problem with marriage is people rush into it blindly, without forethought. Agreeing to live together for...

TIZZY. ... the children's sake? (*Short pause.*)

GOODSELL. I told you, Tizzy, what's good for us is good for him. (*Popping an M&M.*) You sure you don't want... ? (*Offering.*)

TIZZY. No, thank you.

GOODSELL. Divorce is a carefully weighed decision. Mutually satisfying.

TIZZY. Still...

GOODSELL. Still?

TIZZY. The boy.

GOODSELL. The boy?

TIZZY. He's confused. At school they emphasize cooperation. Staying on task.

GOODSELL. (*Dismissive.*) Day care.

TIZZY. Conventional thinking. We all start with conventional thinking.

GOODSELL. Who's more conventional than us?

TIZZY. (*Standing.*) They say he's being uncooperative.

GOODSELL. Good.

TIZZY. (*Holding out the non-toxic apple.*) They say he's not a bird lover.

GOODSELL. He's a Goodsell. We don't go in for birds. You start feeding the birds and what happens? They become dependant on it. Next thing you know, you'll have more birds than you can handle. They'll be flocking in, looking for a hand out. That's not what I expect them to be teaching my son. I expect them to be teaching him self-reliance, self-sufficiency, self-motivation. That's the natural way of things. For the birds. And for Goodsells.

TIZZY. Still...

GOODSELL. Still?

TIZZY. I'm his mother.

GOODSELL. And I'm his father. A father who knows that care needs to be managed. Care isn't something you bestow on everybody. You don't squander care universally. Care needs to be selective. The way I care for you. There are always terms, Tizzy. Who knows that better than us?

TIZZY. All I'm saying is we need to be setting a good example.

GOODSELL. Good? You think the admissions office of Nichols, McLaughlin & Murray is interested in recruiting good? You think they're interested in good boys. Good isn't good enough. Good gets you waiting listed. Day care mentality needs to stay in day care.

TIZZY. Still...

GOODSELL. We're contending with a legacy situation. Gender and ethnic balancing. There are already thirty kids enrolled in the Nichols, McLaughlin & Murray Beginners' class and, if all of them return for kindergarten positions, that'll leave only three openings for the one hundred or so applicants for fall semester. Three!

TIZZY. Competition.

GOODSELL. Natural selection.

TIZZY. For the fortunate few.

GOODSELL. Individual achievement is the only way, Tizzy. It's the example we set. (*Popping another M&M and looking at his empty hand.*) Hey, look! Melts in your mouth not in your hands. (*Holding up his hands for Tizzy to see.*) As advertised. (*Goodsell goes to his desk.*)

GOODSELL. We'll need to find a replacement for Bernie. I'm thinking of a lateral promotion. Keeping the job in house. I prefer it when people climb the ladder, but...

TIZZY. The loss of a father hurts. It leaves a hole. (*Goodsell stops. He turns.*)

GOODSELL. Still?

TIZZY. Still.

GOODSELL. I'm the best provider I can be.

TIZZY. Care, Nellie. He needs for you to care. He needs ...

GOODSELL. Us?

TIZZY. (*Nods.*) Still. (*Goodsell walks over and picks up the game box and looks at it for the first time.*)

GOODSELL. Non-competitive play. (*Looking up from the game box.*) Would be nice, wouldn't it, Tizzy? If it all came down to the goodness of our hearts, it would be ...

TIZZY. Nice?

GOODSELL. Yeah. (*Curtain.*)

* * *

TESTIMONY

by

William Donnelly

Testimony premiered at the First Annual Boston Theater Marathon on April 18th, 1999. Sponsored by Merrimack Repertory Theatre. Directed by David Kent. The cast was as follows:

MAN .... Ken Baltin
VOICE 1 .... Joe Smith
VOICE 2 .... Bill Mootos

For HDM

CHARACTERS

MAN — a man in his forties
VOICE 1 — the same
VOICE 2 — a man in his fifties
VOICE 3 — the same*

*NOTE: In the BTM production, the roles of VOICE 1 and VOICE 3 were played by the same actor.

TIME
Present

PLACE
A room suitable for a legal proceeding

TESTIMONY

(The Man is dressed in a dark suit, seated. The Voices are unseen, speaking into microphones.)

VOICE 1. ... and what was the nature of this meeting ... ?

MAN. ... the nature ... ?

VOICE 1. You were saying before...

MAN. I ... yes ... I'm sorry...

VOICE 2. You were telling us the nature of the meeting.

MAN. Right. Right. Yes. I'd just like to consult my notes if I may ...

VOICE 1. Please.

MAN. *(Flipping through pages in a file.)* I'm just trying to ... Ah! Oh. No.

VOICE 2. Sir...

MAN. Yes. I'm ... As you can see...

VOICE 2. If you'd like to know what you said, I can tell you what you said. I have it right here in front of me. From your deposition on the twenty first: *(Reading.)* "We may have been alone. I can't say for sure. It's entirely possible. We were there, in my office, and she was asking me about Christmas. What the policy for Christmas was. And I'm sure I must have told her because I don't recall hearing any more about it." *(Pause.)* So you met her...

MAN. Where do you see that?

VOICE 2. Page forty-eight.

MAN. ... forty-eight...

VOICE 2. You arranged for a meeting and she met you.

MAN. No. No. It's difficult to understand if you don't ... She came to me with a concern...

VOICE 2. ... and you met her in the presence of whom? (*Pause.*)

VOICE 1. Sir?

MAN. Yes.

VOICE 1. The gentleman is asking you: Were you alone?

MAN. (*Pause.*) Well this is where the matter becomes difficult. The thing it comes down to ... and I don't know if you wish to consider it semantics or ... etymology even. But. The term "alone"— and let me try to state this properly. "Alone" does not mean only one thing. Now. The question seems to be, if I'm not mistaken, did she ... did —

VOICE 2. ... the girl ...

MAN. The woman. Yes. Is who I'm referencing. The woman. Did she, in her own conception of the encounter, consider us, as you say, "alone"? Well. Perhaps she did. At the very least, she says she did. She obviously thought she was. Now. Is that the case? From her standpoint—sure, there was no one else around— Well, no. Let me try and clarify that. Not that there was no one else "around," but that there was no one outwardly visible. Okay? No one there was visible. Now, for me, from my standpoint ... I felt, personally, that, indeed there was a feeling of privacy, but, in acknowledging the pliancy of the word, were we, in fact "alone"— I would say no. And being that we weren't alone —

VOICE 2. But, sir, you said in your previous statement ...

MAN. ... I said, "We may have been alone."

VOICE 2. (*Reading.*) "...we may have been alone. I can't say for sure. It's entirely possible," is what you said.

MAN. Exactly. Yes.

VOICE 1. "It's entirely possible."

MAN. Possible but not definite.

VOICE 2. But you saw it as definite.

MAN. No, I saw it as possible. You're presuming I saw it as definite.

VOICE 2. So what is the truth of that statement?

MAN. The truth. Is. Well...

VOICE 1. The truth is that you saw it as possible but not definite.

MAN. ... which is why in my previous statement I chose to use the word possible and not definite, yes.

VOICE 1. If I may go back for a moment ... You said of the encounter that you were in private, but not alone.

MAN. I said I felt there was privacy.

VOICE 2. So you were alone.

MAN. No, I said I felt privacy.

VOICE 1. Could... ?   VOICE 2. This is...

MAN. The nature of my position ... If you were to ask me "Was I alone" ... well, I'm never alone. There's always ...   No matter what the outward appearance in regards to the goings on in my office is ... that is to say ... no matter how "alone" I may appear ...   I'm never ... adhering to the letter of the definition ... alone. What I mean to say is ... there's always someone around. But even when there is someone, as there always is, I can still exact a certain measure of, as I said, privacy, and indeed, in those moments I can feel private, regardless of my actual "aloneness" which — if you'll allow — is defined by the absence of prying eyes. To my mind anyway. (*Pause.*)

Does that ... ?
VOICE 2. So, in the absence of prying eyes...
MAN. That is correct, sir.
VOICE 2. I haven't asked my question.
MAN. Beg your pardon, sir.
VOICE 2. In the absence of prying eyes ... in those moments where there are, in your words, an absence of prying eyes ... are you, in your mind, in those moments, alone?
MAN. Well ... see ... no. But I am in private.
VOICE 2. Sir...
MAN. No, you...
VOICE 2. The question is...
MAN. If you'd listen to what I'm saying...
VOICE 2. I'm trying to listen to what you're saying...
MAN. See ... she ... the confounding thing here is ... when two people are asked to define a moment — Look ... I can tell you, "Yes, this is what happened." Right? I can do that quite easily. And, thus far, if I may, I feel that I have done that to the best of my ability. But if she says "No"—or if anyone else steps forward and says "No"—then how can you say definitely that they were right and I was wrong? This isn't a matter of sequence we're dealing with. This is all very subjective. And, as we all know ... there is always the variable of slant in these things ... of nuance, and ... Okay. If she felt we were alone, but I felt something less so, then you tell me, were we alone or were we not? You can't say. Do you see what I'm saying? If she says— There's a depth of subtlety here. I work ... in the way that I work ... If I read the situation differently than someone else, then ... I don't know ... if that's unpardonable...
VOICE 2. Excuse me, the issue is not...

MAN. May I finish?

VOICE 1. Sir...

VOICE 2. The issue is not ... no ... the issue is not what is pardonable and what is unpardonable. The issue is ... The issue...

VOICE 3. The issue is: What have you told us, and what have you willfully not told us? (*Pause.*)

VOICE 1. Sir? (*Pause.*) Sir?

MAN. Have you ever seen a girl and just known you were supposed to be inside her? I mean, you just knew she was gonna let you in? Well, this girl was there, you know? She was all there. From the first day she came in. You could see the newness on her. Twenty-one, twenty-two. They don't even know at that age. They're still fresh. Fresh as pie. They got those bright eyes. Bright mouth. Ass all high and rounded. And I'll always look at a mouth. Try and find out what those lips are saying. How they wrap themselves around her words. And this mouth wanted to go, boy, let me tell ya. It was ready to take it all.

So, I played with her for a while. Flirted. Oh, she liked to play. It was her favorite. I'd tease her. She'd tease back. We'd throw looks across the office. She let me know it was time.

I took her in back. She locked the door. She smiled for a second, that smile. She opened her blouse. Put my hands on her. And she was firm—her breasts. And the nipples were stiff. She pressed me hard up against her and still she stayed firm. You could feel how young she was.

"What can I do?" she said. I'm looking at my hands on her skin. "I want to do everything she won't do," she said, 'cause she knew my wife did nothing.

Then she lifted her skirt. She was bare. She pulled my hands real slow down her belly. And I saw her line. Beneath the line it was whiter; between her legs. And then back onto the thighs it was less white. But she wasn't shaved. I don't mean to give you that impression. She was all natural and that's the way I like it. Natural.

She led my hands all the way down and I could finally smell the musk. Maybe not musk, but it was deep like that. And clean. And she was already wet. She was on. She put my mouth up to her. Into her heat. And her froth. She was moving all around. We were moving with her breathing. Then she wanted to turn around. She wanted to put it up in front of me. And you know when it's right there in front of you, what can you do? I moistened my finger. I slid it in. Then deeper. Then she asked for everything.

I waited for a second. Then I gave her everything. When she's asking, you gotta give it to her, am I right?

So I'm pulsing and I'm working it. I get all the way in. And I wanted to keep going. I wanted to disappear. I wanted to see how long she could hold me 'cause you know how they can do that? When they're tight? Well, she was tight, boy. She was strong. She held me in there, and she held it 'til I couldn't hardly wait anymore. And then she let go. Then it flooded.

I was shaking. All my muscles. My legs. I was shaking like I was frightened for my life. But I wasn't frightened. I was lit up.

She turned back around. She took it up. She kissed it. My penis, you know? She put it in her mouth and she kissed it even though it was dead and shrinking away.

Then I offered her my handkerchief. She wiped herself out. I asked for it back. I still have it. I still carry it. It kept her scent.

So that was that time and then there were others. But as I said, we may not have been alone. Some people like to watch. (*Pause.*) So. Do you find that helpful? (*There is a long silence. Perhaps we hear a throat clear over the microphone. The lights go black.*)

* * *

THE YELLOW BUS

by

Leslie Epstein

The Yellow Bus was produced at the First Annual Boston Theater Marathon on April 18th, 1999. Sponsored by Boston Playwrights Theatre. Directed by Daniel Gidron. The cast was as follows:
LIPICZANY .... Joe Smith

CHARACTERS

NISEL LIPICZANY — is a boy of, let us say, fourteen. He has returned to the Lodz Ghetto in 1942, after witnessing the scene he describes in The Yellow Bus.

THE YELLOW BUS

(*Nisel Lipiczany has escaped from a trainload of Jews who were sent from the Ghetto and told they were being sent to a farm. He has followed the train tracks for days, and at last come to their terminus. Now he has returned to the Ghetto to tell his story*)

NISEL. I arrived late in the night. The tracks curved off side by side into a forest. The woods — was it from my fever? — they seemed enchanted. The rails gleamed like the path left by a pair of giant snails. And there was the moon, sitting in the branches like a bright, fat owl. I plunged in.

But soon the trees stopped. Cut down. The rails continued to the age of the clearing. There was a stream there. It made a gushing sound. And another sound, a groaning, a creaking. It came from a building, a big one, made from wood. All around it were the Death's-Headers. The Totenkopfers! They were sitting and smoking and walking this way, that way, this way. The moonlight moved on their helmets. On that spot, in that hiding place, I fell asleep for the night.

Dawn. Dawn, Jews! Dawn of a day. Now I could see everything in the clearing. The mill had three stories. A peaked roof. And a water wheel at one end. Turning and turning. I could see how the black buckets, the wet buckets, rose out of and sank into the roof. This was the noise, the creaking, I heard in the night. I lay pressed to the ground. The sky above was full of dark, low clouds, like sacks of something about to burst. What was this place? Why were the windows of the mill boarded up? What — could someone tell me what — was it grinding? Then a Warrior — he pulled on gloves, white ones, lifted the bar on the door and some of the Jews came out.

There were thirty of them all together. They carried their bundles. They still had their stars on their coats. It was a small group, not even one carload, but the Warrior was already shutting the door behind their backs. No more came out. The Jews started to march across the clearing. Where were they going? I plunged deeper into the forest and began to run in the same direction. It seemed to take forever! I tripped on roots. Branches, like whips, struck my head, my face. By the time I reached the other end of the clearing, the Jews had already arrived. They stood about in their black coats, their black hats. The Death's-Headers were standing, too, or leaning against the side of an old yellow bus.

The front of this bus was pointed toward me — no, not toward me exactly but toward a kind of gully, a dried-up riverbed, a little to my left. I could see the old-fashioned round headlights, one cracked, the other without a lens at all. The wings of the hood were lifted and a Warrior was lying over the fender, at work on the engine inside. The yellow roof — it was battered, dented, as if it had been stoned.

THE YELLOW BUS 59

The band of Jews moved closer to the rear of the bus. They were all from our courtyard. I knew the names of many in the crowd: Palfinger, a jeweler, two of the Fiebig sons, the Widow Greenkraut. And there, Madam Dickstein — I saw her black hair in a bun and the small, white bundle in her hand. I thought: Here they are, the plowers, the milkmaids, the ones who will pluck up the eggs. This is the bus that will take them all the way to the farm.

Then one of the Lords and Masters said something to them. Right away the Jews put down their sacks and valises and began to take off their clothes. Everything. All of it. Even the undergarments. And they tied their shoes together by the laces.

How white they were! Whiter than birches! How thin! In my life I had not seen a grown person completely without clothes. Some of the women, some men, kept their hands in front of their bodies. But the rest — the rest: it was a shock to me to see the black hair, especially the women's hair, growing between their legs, and far up their bellies. The back door of the bus swung open, the thirty Jews climbed inside, and the door slammed shut once more.

Nothing happened. The Blond Ones stood here and there, with their arms crossed or with their fingers in their belts. Finally, the mechanic slid from the fender, clapped — like this! — his hands together, and turned the crank. The engine started. The bus body shook. One half the hood slammed down and the other half banged against itself.

Drive off! Drive away! Drive to the farm! But the old bus did not move from the spot.

Only then, then, did I noticed two things: first, that the front wheels were missing, and second — there was no driver on the seat inside. Can you blame me if I thought this must be a dream? A coach without wheels, with no one to drive it: yet the engine roars, the body shakes, it sways, as if it speeding along a highway. Minutes went by, one like another. A dark bird, dark like a crow, floated downward from the sky. It perched on top of Madame Dickstein's white bundle. The motor ran for a quarter of an hour. But it was the bird that scared me. Horrible! As tame as a person's pet.

Then the engine stopped and they took the Jews out of the bus. All of them — Mister Palfinger and Adolph Fiebig and the rest — were sleeping.

Horses now. White horses. They came up from the direction of the mill. They were pulling a rubber-wheeled cart. In this cart the Pabianice Jews were driven away. Where? Up the dried up riverbed. Out of sight. The piles of clothing, the luggage, the shoes — that remained behind.

And now, one after the other came fresh groups of Jews. The bus shuddered as usual, and then the sleepers were brought out again. Once with Jews still on board, something went wrong with the engine. It ran. Then it stopped. How pleasant it was. How peaceful. A Man of Valor — it was the same one with the gloves, the one from the mill: he walked to the side of the bus and put his ear against it. *Just like in a synagogue.* That's what he said. Then they cranked the engine and the old omnibus — did those inside think they were on a journey, going past fields and forests and towns? — returned to life. Shaking.

THE YELLOW BUS

Shaking.

Finally, at dusk, the rubber-wheeled cart picked up the mountain of clothing. The Warriors walked beside it to the mill.

Night fell. No stars. No moon. It was as dark as it is when I have my eyes shut. I walked into the riverbed. There were pebbles, smooth ones, round ones. I could feel them through my shoes. After a while, not long, a few minutes, I came to where the Jews were lying. Too dark to see their faces. Impossible to tell if my mother or father or Gutta and Nelli were there. This is what I said: I said, *Wake up! Wake up, Jews! Let's go back to the ghetto! I know the way!* But they didn't wake up. No. It was I who fell asleep beside them instead.

In the morning my mind was clear. Sane. Rational. Before I opened my eyes, I knew I would be surrounded by corpses. And there — there they were. With excrement on their legs. And some of the women stained with their own blood. I heard a sound. Not the creak-creak-creak of the millwheel. Not the way the autobus went R-R-R-R-R-R-R-R and Bang! Bang! Bang! No. This was soft. Nice almost. *Shhhhh. Shhhhh.* Like someone with his finger on his lips. *Shhhhh.* I looked around. Two men were walking among the bodies. They were bending like farmers with scythes. They cut off the locks of the dead people's hair.

What else to do but jump up and run? Run! Up the riverbank, through the clearing, into the forest. Then south, always south, not once stopping — until I came to where I thought there would be Jews. And I succeeded. I arrived.

(A very brief pause: then, to the audience.)

Isn't it true? Aren't you? Look at me, dear people! All of you people! Are you awake? Are you alive? Are you Jews?

* * *

TAKING ROOT

by

Chapin Garner

THE BOSTON THEATER MARATHON

Taking Root premiered at the First Annual Boston Theater Marathon on April 18th, 1999. Sponsored by Jewish Theatre of New England. Directed by Will Lyman. The cast was as follows:

MAN #1 .... Lonnie Farmer
MAN #2 .... John Morgan

For Kate Snodgrass – Thank you
for Your Vision, Passion, Care, and Support.
You are a gift and blessing to our community.

TAKING ROOT

(A field. The stage is bare. Man 1 is kneeling on the ground with his eyes closed and his cheek pressed against the ground. He is a black man in his mid-forties. He is neatly dressed in tan slacks, a white oxford shirt, and a windbreaker. A folded lawn chair lays on the ground next to him. He inhales deeply, taking pleasure in the scented air. He takes a number of deep and pleasurable breaths, and then slowly opens his eyes out in the direction of the audience. At his own time and pace he surveys his surroundings with a hint of satisfaction. He opens up the lawn chair, sets it on the ground and then sits down in it. He casually takes in his surroundings again and then closes his eyes. He takes another deep breath. Man 2 approaches Man 1 from offstage. Man 2 is an Irishman in his late sixties. He wears a green, one-piece gardener's suit. He has a shovel slung over his shoulder. He appears to be a hearty and well weathered old man. His clothes are stained with dirt and grass.)

MAN 2. 'Scuse me, sir.
Man 1. *(Startled, but still peaceful.)* Yes?
MAN 2. We're gonna be needin' to have our truck come through here.

MAN 1. Right here?
MAN 2. We got a service.
MAN 1. I'll keep out of your way.
MAN 2. It'll be comin' any minute. 'Sides it's gonna rain. Supposed ta come down in buckets.
MAN 1. Fifteen years living here... I'm used to it. Give it twenty minutes. It'll change. I'll be on the lookout for the truck – and the rain. Promise.
MAN 2. This yer spot?
MAN 1. Thinking about it. I'm checking out a couple locations.
MAN 2. This is one of the... it's someone else's spot. Sure you're in the right place?
MAN 1. I thought — perhaps I'm turned around. (*Pulls a piece of paper and hands it to Man 2. Man 2 studies the paper carefully.*) Am I?
MAN 2. Don't make no sense. This is another fella's spot. Always has been.
MAN 1. They said it was available.
MAN 2. Can't be right.
MAN 1. I'm just telling you what they told me.
MAN 2. I don't understand it — I ain't gonna argue with 'em. (*Pause.*) It's a shame, though.
MAN 1. A shame?
MAN 2. They suggested other spots to ya?
MAN 1. I think I like this ridge best. Nice view.
MAN 2. You gonna be seein' much the day you take this spot? Wouldn't be my choice.
MAN 1. No?
MAN 2. Lotta traffic through here. Busiest place we got. People parade right through here — don't bother to look where their steppin'. Grass gets all trampled. See how it's brownin'?

TAKING ROOT

MAN 1. It looks well kept to me.

MAN 2. Don't look too close. Anywhere. This is a hellava big place. Can hardly keep up with it.

MAN . How many people does it take — to keep up with it?

MAN 2. More 'an we got.

MAN 1. How many of there are you?

MAN 2. Yer lookin' at the crew.

MAN 1. No.

MAN 2. That's right. Everyday for the last forty-three years.

MAN 1. How? You must have... what... three hundred acres?

MAN 2. Three hundred twenty-seven. That's just the fields. We can expand another hundred and ninety inta the woods over there.

MAN 1. You mow this whole place yourself?

MAN 2. (*Man 1 nods.*) That's right. And no ridin' mower neither. I push it.

MAN 1. That's... this whole place yourself?

MAN 2. Believe it.

MAN 1. That must take forever.

MAN 2. I do a bit each day.

MAN 1. Bet you're glad you don't have stones.

MAN 2. I'm old fashioned that way. Like stones. Wish we had 'em.

MAN 1. You'd have to mow around each one.

MAN 2. Place's got no character, if ya ask me. Not the way it is. What do I know...

MAN 1. That's why I chose this place. It's like one great big field. A meadow. I love the cleared ground. Rich, dark soil. The smell... (*Man 1 inhales deeply, and shuts his eyes for a moment.*) But now, to think of you...

it's not inexpensive to get in here. They must have the money to hire who they want.

MAN 2. Don't have to tell me. And what happens as result? Huh?

MAN 1. What?

MAN 2. Nothin'.

MAN 1. What?

MAN 2. I shouldn't. Not if yer sold on it already.

MAN 1. I'm not sold on anything. Not yet.

MAN 2. I can't. (*In a whisper.*) They'd have my head. This ain't much, but it's a job.

MAN 1. I wouldn't mention anything to anyone.

MAN 2. (*Pause.*) I don't know. If you choose to go someplace else...I can't be responsible for that.

MAN 1. It would be helpful. This is a big decision. (*Pause.*) What happens here?

MAN 2. (*Pause.*) If it's gonna be a help... Ya swear you won't whisper a word to nobody?

MAN 1. I swear.

MAN 2. (*Man 2 looks around to see if anyone is in earshot.*) It's about what doesn't happen 'round here. A lotta things just don't get done. Important things. I tell 'em we need more help, do they listen to me?

MAN 1. Important things?

MAN 2. (*Looks around to see if anyone is within earshot.*) Last month I was mowin' by those willas over there. There was a service — who tells me? Not a soul. You know how hard it is to put a box in the ground with no hole bein' dug?   MAN 1. You've got to be kidding.

MAN 2. God's honest truth. What a mess. Family's there. Funeral director. Everybody. No hole. No set up — Two years ago we had these five services in one day. All the sudden the sky opens up — started comin' down in buckets — never seen anything like it in my life. I couldn't fill the holes quick enough. The last one I get to — now by this time I can't see nothin' it's got so late. I get there... It's fulla water. It's filled and overflowin'. I don't know what ta do. I ain't got no help. Can't see a Goddamn thing... I start shovelin' mud inta the hole. I get done with it and it's like quick sand. I go ta sleep fearin' somebody's gonna fall in and get swallowed up, right? Next mornin' I go to check it out. It looks as if things are dryin' up a bit. I make my way to the last hole I filled the night before. Who's there but the dead fella's daughter. She's talkin' to 'im – leavin' 'im flowers. I start to walk away, but then, outa the corner of my eye I see this casket lying on it's side down by the brook over there. It's open and guess who's lying on the ground?

MAN 1. That can't happen.

MAN 2. Most certainly did!

MAN 1. How?

MAN 2. (*Man 1 shrugs.*) Hole musta filled with water... the box rose to the top and then floated its way down to the brook. (*Pause.*) Traffic aside. This ain't all that bad a location. However, down by the pine grove ... if I could choose anyplace to be – that's the spot. Shady. Quiet. Nobody to bother ya.

MAN 1. Have you told them? About... what isn't getting done around here.

MAN 2. They know. Did they suggest any spots by the pine grove?

MAN 1. No one cares?

MAN 2. I'm used to it. What do ya want me to say?

MAN 1. I can't do this. Not if what your saying is... does anyone else know about this? The families? Visitors? Someone must have seen something — if it's as bad as you say.

MAN 2. See. I shouldn't of said nothin'. Yer all bent outa shape now. Just forget what I said. Check those spots down by the pines. You'll like it better down there. Trust me.

MAN 1. Forget about it? Could you be buried here knowing what you know? Could you?

MAN 2. I... not by choice — no.

MAN 1. Exactly. You've been very helpful. Don't worry. I'm... I'm... I don't know what to say.

MAN 2. Don't say nothin'.

MAN 1. I won't. Well this... where do I go from here? (*Pause.*) Any suggestions? You must have the inside track. Where is your final resting place going to be?

MAN 2. I'm stuck here. It's free. They call it perk.

MAN 1. I'm not so sure.

MAN 2. Tell me 'bout it.

MAN 1. Are you down by the pines?

MAN 2. (*Pause.*) No. I don't get much choice in the matter.

MAN 1. Where are you going to be?

MAN 2. (*Pause.*) Just a... a little ways down from here.

MAN 1. Where?

MAN 2. (*Points to a spot only a few steps away from where Man 1 is standing.*) There.

MAN 1. Here? I thought this was —

MAN 2. I told ya — didn't have much choice in the matter. You should see the yella jackets in the summer. Some reason this spot is swarmin' with 'em. Ain't nobody gonna be visitin' me here in the summer, that's for darn sure!

MAN 1. Yellow jackets, huh? Hardly seems fair – with all the work you do here.

TAKING ROOT 71

MAN 2. You ain't sayin' nothin' I haven't thought a thousand times meself! Check inta Cedar Grove or Calvary. Good places. Well maintained. Don't cost a fortune neither. Not like this place. (*Pause. Man 1 looks at Man 2 suspiciously.*) That truck's gonna be comin' in pretty soon. We're gonna need to be getting' to work — the service.

MAN 1. Yes. Of course. Thank you. Cedar Grove, Calvary?

MAN 2. That's right. Either one'd suit ya well, I suspect.

MAN 1. South of town?

MAN 2. Uh-huh. Good luck to ya now.

MAN 1. (*Folds up his lawn chair. Man 2 begins to leave.*) I'm sorry to bother you... but... I'm curious... who's we?

MAN 2. What's that?

MAN 1. Who's we?

MAN 2. We?

MAN 1. Yes. The truck. Whose driving the truck in?

MAN 2. Shamus. Not that I got much business given his name out.

MAN 1. To prepare for the service?

MAN 2. That's right. My right hand man.

MAN 1. You've got to dig the hole, things like that?

MAN 2. And set up for the service. There's a lot ta do and I'm a afraid we're gonna have to be getting' to it. Been nice talkin' with ya. (*Continues to leave.*)

MAN 1. As soon as he gets here.

MAN 2. Which'll be any moment now. So I should get started.

MAN 1. I thought you worked alone. The only one taking care of the place. (*Long pause.*) This Shamus doesn't count as part of your crew? Your crew of one.

MAN 2. (*Long pause. Man 2 chuckles.*) I'll be damned. Not so slow as I thought. How can I make it clearer to ya... (*Pause. Man 2 begins to point at different plots.*) Grew up with them. Those folks lived down the block. That fella was my father's best friend. And that lady, that lady was my second grade teacher. (*He puts his hand on his chest indicating himself, while pointing at another plot.*) And me. I can go on. Or do I have ta? Down by the pines is my suggestion. Or someplace else. (*Pause.*) This is our ridge.

MAN 1. I appreciate the clarity.

MAN 2. Glad to offer it to ya.

MAN 1. In fact, you've helped me make up my mind. (*Man 1 begins to point out plots Man 2 had pointed at.*) All your you're friends here. (*He points at Man 2's plot.*) You. (*He points at the plot he is standing on.*) And, me. (*Pause.*) We're going to be neighbors. And for a good long time. Unless, of course, you want to move. Down to the pines perhaps. I bet the folks here would agree to that — if you pressed them enough. (*Extremely long uneasy pause.*) I need to go make out a check. Excuse me. (*Man 1 begins to exit.*)

MAN 2. That's how it's gonna be?

MAN 1. Yes.

MAN 2. You folks are always movin' inta our neighborhoods. Makes all of us want to move out. It's a crime.

MAN 1. (*Referring to the plots around him.*) I don't imagine your pals here are going to be doing any relocating in the near future.

MAN 2. This ain't gonna happen. Not on my watch.

MAN 1. No? What are you going to do? Hmm? It's

TAKING ROOT

a done deal. Get used to it... or move out of the neighborhood.

MAN 2. You son-of-a...

MAN 1. You do keep this place quite nice. I think might suggest it to some of my friends. Now that would suit me!

MAN 2. It'll be worse for ya. That's a promise.

MAN 1. You want to test me? Is that it? I'll make this a crusade. That's right. I will yell and holler until the whole city takes notice. We can get loud about this. Real loud. We'll picket this place. Camp out right here on top of... (*Looks at the ground.*)...on top of your second grade teacher! The papers will eat it up. We'll have the Mayor down here. You'll be famous! A celebrity. You're employers will be thrilled with you. You'll be able to tell the entire world how this is your ridge. What would you think of that? (*Long uneasy pause.*) You're going to have to speak up, I can't hear you. (*Pause.*) Hmm?

MAN 2. (*Pause.*) How you plannin' ta go?

MAN 1. What?

MAN 2. Urn or a box?

MAN 1. (*Pause.*) I haven't given it much thought.

MAN 2. Ashes. My suggestion.

MAN 1. (*Pause.*) You're point?

MAN 2. No point. Just less diggin' for somebody ta do. That's how I'm goin'. (*Pause.*) Might want to take that under consideration when yer doin' yer plannin'. (*Pause.*) It's a good spot. Take in the sunset from here some evenin'. Nothin' like it.

MAN 1. (*Pause.*) I'll have to do that... sometime. (*Long uneasy pause. Man 2 exits. Long pause. Man 1 exits in the opposite direction.*)

***

FLAG GIRLS

by

Laura Harrington

76 THE BOSTON THEATER MARATHON

Flag Girls premiered at the First Annual Boston Theater Marathon on April 18th, 1999. Sponsored by Wellesley Theatre Company. Directed by Nora Hussey. The cast was as follows:

AGNES' FATHER .... James Butterfield
SUSIE .... Emily Coddington
MARY JANE .... Lesley Halperin
AGNES .... Elana Hayasaka
MILDRED .... Sasha Pfau
HARRIET .... Erika Reinfeld

CHARACTERS

SUSIE JOHNSON
MARY JANE BARCLAY
HARRIET LEE
AGNES GREEN
MILDRED SOMMERS

TIME
Memorial Day, 1905.

PLACE
Richmond, Virginia.

FLAG GIRLS

(Backstage at the Memorial Day celebration. Five fourteen year old girls are each wrapped in the stripes of the American flag so that, standing together, they create one flag. The Flag Girls are waiting for their cue to come onto the podium for the finale. The girl on the left, (Susie Johnson.) has the stars on her part of the flag. Their arms are pinned inside the flags. Their steps are severely shortened by the narrowness of the flag. This is a U.S. flag, not a confederate or Union flag.)

SUSIE. Quit wriggling, Mary Jane!
MJ. I wish I'd gotten the star part.
AGNES. I wanted the star part.
MILDRED. Everybody wants the star part.
MJ. Susie Johnson always gets the star part because her father's the mayor.
SUSIE. No, I always get the star part because of my superior poise and elocution.
HARRIET. I don't see what elocution has to do with it.
MJ. I got an itch. It's on my nose.
I can't reach it. Now it's on my ear! Oh, no!!
SUSIE. Quit wriggling, Mary Jane!
MJ. I can't help it!
SUSIE. Yes, you can. Now, stop it!

77

MJ. I'm gonna tell on you, Susie Johnson. You always act like butter wouldn't melt in your mouth, but deep down, you are just plain mean.

HARRIET. I hate Memorial Day.

MILDRED. All those smelly old men.

SUSIE. That is disrespectful!

MILDRED. Smelly old men with long hairs coming out of their noses –

HARRIET. They all want kisses.

MILDRED. Those big old beards. Stained with tobacco juice.

MJ. Who wants to remember a dumb war we LOST?

SUSIE. I'm going to report you to Mrs Hill —

HARRIET. They all love to come out and march — shuffle along more like it —

SUSIE. I can't believe this kind of talk from the Flag Girls!!

MJ. Carry those tin trumpets for their ears cause they can't hear no more.

HARRIET. But they sure can pinch good.

AGNES. Oh, no! You got to get my arms free or else there's no hope for me. I'll be black and blue from my nose to my shoes.

MJ. I can't believe they let Susie Johnson sing Dixie. She can't even carry the tune!

SUSIE. If you don't want to be a Flag Girl, you should resign your commission. There are dozens of girls who would give their eye teeth to take your place.

HARRIET. My father said he'd be damned —

SUSIE. You watch your mouth! We are the FLAG GIRLS!

HARRIET. — Damned if he'd sit and listen to the Battle Hymn of the Republic. You watch. When they start that

FLAG GIRLS 79

he's gonna get up off the podium and walk away.

AGNES. Why?

SUSIE. I believe we're going to have to start levying fines for infractions of the Rules. In the meantime, you take that back, Harriet Lee.

HARRIET. Take what back?

SUSIE. That bad language. We are the Flag Girls. We are supposed to set an example.

HARRIET. An example of what, may I ask?

SUSIE. If you don't know, you really don't belong with the Flag Girls.

HARRIET. Is this some knowledge I'm supposed to have been born with?

SUSIE. My granddaddy died in the War Between the States. This is very real to me and mine.

MJ. My granddaddy died, too.

AGNES. My granddaddy's Jewish.

SUSIE. (*Consoling her.*) That's all right, Agnes, honey.

MILDRED. So what does that have to do with us? We're not our granddaddies are we?

SUSIE. It's what we believe.

MILDRED. And what is that, exactly?

SUSIE. This war isn't over.

HARRIET. Really.

AGNES. Come on, Susie, you don't really think that. You're just saying what your parents say.

MILDRED. It is so hot in here! Don't you think it's hot in here? I swear, I am perspiring to beat the band – This ol flag is gonna slide right off me –

MJ. (*She wriggles worse than ever.*)

SUSIE. For the last time, Mary Jane, quit wriggling! You're enough to drive a person crazy!

HARRIET. Mary Jane, you didn't —
MJ. No! I didn't. You can't blame me —
HARRIET. You brought that animal in here.
MJ. Jeb Stuart is not an animal. He's a pet.
AGNES. You brought Jeb Stuart?!?
MJ. No, I didn't!
HARRIET. Yes, you did. I can smell him!
MILDRED. Who's Jeb Stuart, for heaven's sake?
HARRIET. Mary Jane's pet —
MJ. — Don't say it, Harriet!
HARRIET. Snake. (*Susie screams.*)
MILDRED. You have a snake in the flag with you? Where?
AGNES. I can't stand snakes!
SUSIE. You named a snake Jeb Stuart??!! How could you?
MJ. He's a wonderful snake. Very dashing. Just like Jeb.
MILDRED. I have to go to the bathroom
AGNES. I think I'm going to faint.
HARRIET. Where is Jeb Stuart, exactly?
MJ. Around my waist.
SUSIE. Mary Jane you get that snake out of the flag right now.
MJ. (*She tries to wriggle her hands around inside the flag. This is difficult because they're wrapped so tightly. She starts to cry.*)
AGNES. Hurry up!
SUSIE. Mary Jane, you need to stop your crying and do your duty.
MILDRED. Mary Jane, it's always something with you... something wicked and wild and, and, and —
AGNES. How could you bring a snake in here?? I

FLAG GIRLS 81

HATE SNAKES!!

SUSIE. Oh, no! Oh, no! We are falling apart! The Flag Girls cannot fall apart!

AGNES. I think I'm going to throw up!

SUSIE. No! Agnes! Look straight ahead. Take deep breaths. Think of our forefathers. Think of their courage under fire!

HARRIET. If you throw up, Agnes, it will land on your shoes and we will all be sick. Don't do it.

MJ. (*Wails.*) He's gone!

HARRIET. Who?

MJ. (*Sobbing.*) Jeb Stuart!

MILDRED. He's loose?!?!

MJ. (*Falls to her knees.*) Oh, Jeb Stuart, poor Jeb Stuart, where are you?

SUSIE. Mary Jane, I'm afraid you are going to have to leave the flag.

HARRIET. You can't do that, Susie!

AGNES. Listen! You can hear my Daddy talkin'!

SUSIE. We're next, girls! Pull yourselves together.

MARY JANE. Jeb? Jeb Stuart?? Here, boy. Here, Jeb Stuart.

AGNES' FATHER. (*From offstage.*) And you tell me. Have these fundamental questions been answered? (*Mary Jane begins to crawl around — as best she can – looking for Jeb Stuart.*) Have these fundamental issues been put to rest? Have we become one nation with liberty and justice for all?

SUSIE. Mary Jane! You get back here right now or you are out of this flag! This is my final warning!

AGNES' FATHER. (*Offstage.*) Has there been an emancipation?

MILDRED. Agnes, honey, what in the world is he

talking about? (*The girls sidle over to peek from behind the curtain.*)

AGNES' FATHER. (*Offstage.*) Who, finally, is going to bind up this nation? Who, finally, is going to heal these wounds?

HARRIET. They're not clapping.

AGNES. What's the matter with them?

MILDRED. I think he looks very distinguished, Agnes.

AGNES. What's he doing? Can you see him?

HARRIET. He's just sitting back down.

AGNES. Oh.

HARRIET. It's very quiet out there. (*Fanfare.*)

SUSIE. Oh! There's our fanfare!

MJ. I can't find Jeb Stuart!!! (*She starts to unwrap herself from the flag. It's a struggle.*)

SUSIE. Mary Jane! You stop that! Get back on your feet and get over here! (*Fanfare again.*)

MJ. You're not the boss of me, Susie Johnson. I don't even like you.

SUSIE. All this talk! My throat's so dry. I need my atomizer.

HARRIET. Why don't we just let Mildred sing? She's got such a nice voice. Then you don't have to worry about your atomizer, Susie.

SUSIE. The stars of the flag always sings. Not the stripes. The stars. I should not have to explain this to you, Harriet. We've been doing this together for five years. Proudly.

AGNES. I don't feel so proud. To tell you the truth, I feel kind of confused.

SUSIE. Just don't listen to your father, Agnes, and you'll be fine.

MJ. My mother makes me do it.

FLAG GIRLS

MILDRED. Mine, too. Although I wouldn't mind it so much if I could sing.

AGNES. How come nobody ever talks about Appomatox on Memorial Day? (*A beat. They all look at Agnes.*) Peace. You know, the end of the war?

MJ. (*She has finally managed to wriggle her way out of the flag. She stands up slowly, amazed at herself.*) I did it. I did it! I did it!!

SUSIE. That's it, Mary Jane. That is the last straw. You are no longer a Flag Girl. Dismissed!

MJ. Thank you, Susie Johnson! I have been liberated! Now I can go rescue Jeb Stuart. Ladies – (*MJ makes a sweeping bow in the tradition of Jeb Stuart.*) Farewell! (*MJ exits. Fanfare, and the band strikes up "Dixie".*)

SUSIE. Flag Girls! Face front! Chins up! Heads high! Ready, girls! We're on – (*They hop off stage. Music swells.*)

* * *

MIRROR MAN

by

Dan Hunter

86 THE BOSTON THEATER MARATHON

Mirror Man premiered at the First Annual Boston Theater Marathon on April 18th, 1999. Sponsored by American Stage Festival. Directed by Michael Dell'Orto. The cast was as follows:

SHELLY .... Nicole Kempskie
JANELLE .... Pat Karpen
MIRROR MAN .... Peter Haydn

CHARACTERS

MIRROR MAN — is large, shy and brooding with a scarf wrapped around his neck. He wears an old suit coat. His clothes are old, but good, slightly frayed and worn without attention to detail. He carries an old fashioned doctor's valet case. He doesn't enter; he seems to appear on stage. He tries to avoid looking anyone in the eyes except through his mirror. His eyes look like the eyes of a deer caught in the headlights of an oncoming car.

SHELLY — is in her early-twenties working at the coffee shop while attending college at night.

JANELLE — in her thirties, is divorced, working two jobs including the coffee shop, where she has worked for some time.

TIME — The Present.

PLACE — a North American city.

MIRROR MAN

SCENE ONE

(*About 2:15 pm, Shelly is sitting on a stool with her feet propped on the counter by the cash register, reading and eating an apple, unaware that anyone else is in the shop. Mirror Man sits quietly with his back to Shelly.*

After a brief pause, Mirror Man, moving slowly but deliberately, removes a compact mirror case from inside his suit coat, opens it and positions it to watch Shelly over his shoulder. Shelly squirms slightly, but doesn't look up. She feels uncomfortable without knowing why. She swings her feet to the floor and walks, back to Mirror Man, to the window. As she moves, Mirror Man pivots to keep Shelly in view. She checks the window, turns around, and realizes she is being watched. She feels a brief flutter of panic.)

SHELLY. Oh — I didn't see you.

(*Mirror Man freezes. Unsure, she tests him. She moves back to the cash register, feigning nonchalance. Mirror Man pivots as if sighting through a periscope. She pretends to clean the counter, glancing at Mirror Man, but unsuccessfully trying to avoid locking eyes through the mirror. Shelly resumes her seat on her stool, but keeps her feet on the floor. She pulls her book over her face. Black.)*

SCENE TWO

(3:15 pm, the same day. Mirror Man is seated with his back to Shelly, who is hiding behind her book on the stool by the closet door. Janelle enters and performs her pre-shift ritual: she puts her purse into the closet and checks herself in the mirror.)

JANELLE. Hey, Shell. How's it goin'? *(Shelly motions for Janelle to be quiet.)* Another slow day, huh? Well, I brought my TV Guide crosswords. Think we can close early? *(Shelly, motions Janelle to be quiet, pointing over to Mirror Man.)*
SHELLY. *(Whispering.)* Over there.
JANELLE. What?
SHELLY. That guy. Don't look at him.
JANELLE. Yeah, what about him?
SHELLY. He's just sitting there.
JANELLE. Yeah, well, that's what they do. Think one cup of coffee gives them the right to camp out overnight. Why don't you give him the heave-ho? *(Janelle goes back to looking in the closet mirror. Mirror Man has unfolded his compact case, wipes it clean and spies over his*

MIRROR MAN 89

shoulder again.)

SHELLY. He's weird.

JANELLE. Honey, they're all weird. My husband's weird, Bill Clinton's weird. This creep's weird.

SHELLY. Weird weird.

JANELLE. Hey, you're really spooked. How long's he been in here? (*Mirror Man removes the compact mirror case from inside his suit coat, opens it, cleans it with a handkerchief and positions it to watch Shelly over his shoulder.*)

SHELLY. I don't know. An hour, maybe two. Look at him, he's doin' it again.

JANELLE. Doin' what? What's he doin'?

SHELLY. Lookin' at us.

JANELLE. Ignore him. Just a creep tryin' to get some thrills.

SHELLY. He's lookin' at us with that thing.

JANELLE. What thing?

SHELLY. One of those mirror things. Look at him.

JANELLE. I'm not going to look at him. You want I should encourage him?

SHELLY. Let's kick him out. He hasn't had any coffee or anything.

JANELLE. OK, I'll talk to him. (*To Mirror Man.*) Hey, buddy, you going to have any coffee or what? This ain't the bus depot, you know. (*Mirror Man remains still.*)

SHELLY. Don't look at him, Janelle.

JANELLE. Hello? Earth to moon man? Come in, please. (*Mirror Man pivots to fix Janelle in the mirror. Janelle sees his eyes through the mirror and quickly turns away.*)

SHELLY. Did you see his eyes?

JANELLE. (*Pause.*) His eyes. (*As if transported into*

another world.)

SHELLY. See what I mean? It's weird; it's more than weird.

JANELLE. Should we call the cops?

SHELLY. I don't know. Is it against the law to watch people through a mirror?

JANELLE. (*Back to her normal self.*) Call the cops. You don't need a law to tell you when something's too weird.

SHELLY. What are we goin' to say?

JANELLE. That he's a creep. They got a place for creeps.

SHELLY. OK, call 'em.

JANELLE. Why me? He's your guy. It's not even my shift yet.

SHELLY. He's right by the phone. I don't want to go near him. You go.

JANELLE. I'm not going near him.

SHELLY. Wait a minute, I got an idea. (*Louder.*) Call the cops, Janelle.

JANELLE. (*Pauses before she gets it.*) I already did. I think I hear the squad car pullin' up in back now.

SHELLY. The cops are here. (*Louder.*) Hey, the cops are here.

(*Mirror Man quickly slips away, leaving his valet case. Janelle exits, following him to make sure he is gone. Shelly walks over to Mirror Man's abandoned case. She opens it, pulls out some old clothes, and then pulls out a hand-held, oval vanity mirror. Shelly looks at herself in the mirror. Janelle enters.*)

MIRROR MAN 91

JANELLE. I guess he's gone. They didn't see him next door. But, Jack said he'd take care of him, if he comes back. You know Jack? He's kind of cute. Hey, Shelly, whattya doin'?

SHELLY. He left his briefcase.

JANELLE. Well, for God's sake, leave it alone. (*Shelly quickly hides the mirror and closes the valet case.*)

SHELLY. Maybe there's an address or something.

JANELLE. Just throw it away.

SHELLY. You can't just throw it away. He probably wants it.

JANELLE. Ok, Ok. Stick it in the closet, so we don't have to see it. (*Shelly lugs the case over to the closet.*)

SHELLY. Jesus, it weighs a ton. Don't you want to know what's in it?

JANELLE. Why on earth?

SHELLY. I don't know. I mean — what's with the mirror thing anyway?

JANELLE. Who knows? Maybe it was a camera.

SHELLY. Right, and he's a spy. For the CIA, I suppose.

JANELLE. No, he looked more foreign. KGB.

SHELLY. They don't exist anymore.

JANELLE. Are you kidding? That's just what they want you to think.

SHELLY. Then, what's a spy doin' in here?

JANELLE. Spies gotta drink coffee. Maybe he was just testing his secret spy camera.

SHELLY. Weird. Spies in here. Do you think we should tell someone? We got his secret bag.

JANELLE. Right. Then we get locked up as the crackpots. Did you ever see a UFO? Well, take it from me — don't. No matter what you saw, you're the fruitcake.

SHELLY. But, we both saw him in here. Using that mirror thing. It must have been some kind of a ray gun. I could feel something weird — like there was some sort of force field all around him.

JANELLE. Yeah, well, maybe we saw him and maybe we didn't. I'm just saying sometimes it don't pay to open your mouth. You better cash out. (*Janelle goes to the closet to check herself in the mirror.*)

SHELLY. Yeah, you're right. (*Shelly begins counting the money from the cash register. Mirror Man softly enters, sits down in the same seat as if he'd never moved with his back to the cash register.*)

JANELLE. (*From closet.*) You know what Jack said, don't you? He said anyone who'd sit around watching other people is plain nutso and ought to be locked up. (*Moment's pause.*) Hey, did you see the nutsoes they had on Geraldo last night (*Entering.*)... oh-oh... Shelly, he's back.

SHELLY. Oh my God. That's him. What should we do?

JANELLE. I don't know. It's still your shift. Ask him if he wants coffee.

SHELLY. It's self-service.

JANELLE. Maybe he don't know, you know maybe he's from Russia or something. Go on. (*Shelly creeps up behind Mirror Man.*)

SHELLY. Excuse me, may I take your order.

MIRROR MAN. (*Politely but without turning around.*) Half-and-half with coffee. And sugar. Please. (*Shelly retreats, returns with coffee, carefully setting it down without coming in front of him.*)

SHELLY. There you go. Coffee black, half-and-half and I stirred the sugar in for you. (*Mirror Man places one hand on the cup, but doesn't drink. Shelly waits a step or two away. Mirror Man stretches his head slightly upward and toward Shelly, as if to say "do you want something?")*

SHELLY. I'm sorry. Most people pay first, you know.
MIRROR MAN. No, thank you.
SHELLY. You can pay later. It doesn't matter, really. *(She pauses.)* You know that you left your case here? *(Shelly waits for a response. She gives up, returns to Janelle.)*
JANELLE. Well, what do you think?
SHELLY. He's not so bad, maybe. Strong, silent type.
JANELLE. Well, he's not dressed half-bad. Kind of cute, you know, if you like the spy type. *(Mirror Man removes his mirror, staring over his shoulder again.)*
SHELLY. A spy. Do you really think he's a spy?
JANELLE. Well, he's a customer now, so live with it... Wait a minute. Don't look now, it's the mirror bit again.
SHELLY. Go get Jack.
JANELLE. Yeah, ok.
SHELLY. Janelle. Go get Jack. *(Janelle starts, but freezes as Mirror Man pivots to see her.)*
SHELLY. *(Loudly.)* Just go. Hurry. *(Mirror Man is startled, jumps up, looks at the women in fear and scampers out the door.)*
SHELLY. He's gone.
JANELLE. Thank God.
SHELLY. Yeah.
JANELLE. You know, men are always, you know, giving me the eye, but that mirror thing — makes my skin crawl.
SHELLY. Well, maybe it's like he sees something we don't see.
JANELLE. Right. Like that mirror gives him X-ray vision. Honey, Superman — he's not. Look at how he ran

out of here. Like a scared rabbit.

SHELLY. Maybe he just likes to look at everything backwards.

JANELLE. Mirrors do that?

SHELLY. Oh yeah, mirrors turn everything around. Haven't you ever seen the backwards writing on the front of an ambulance? So, you can read it frontwards in your rear-view mirror.

JANELLE. Yeah? So, what's he's doin'? Tryin' to change lanes?

SHELLY. I don't know. But, he's watching us... like we're some kind of show.

JANELLE. Why's he lookin' at us?

SHELLY. He's not lookin' at us. He's lookin' at us backwards.

JANELLE. I don't know. Maybe lookin' backwards through the mirror makes it backwards looking frontwards.

SHELLY. No, see if we do something frontwards, then it's going to look backwards to him. But, if we do something backwards...

JANELLE. Jesus, Shelly, stop it. The guy's a creep. I don't believe you. Ten minutes ago, you were too scared to call the cops.

SHELLY. He's there and he's not there, like he doesn't want us to see him — frontwards.

JANELLE. And he didn't even pay. Wouldn't you know?

SHELLY. That's right. Cuz, see that's backwards. Frontwards he would've paid. (*Black.*)

SCENE THREE

(The next day. Coffee shop. Making sure no one is around, Shelly opens the valet case. She pulls out the clothes, and begins pulling out a series of mirrors. She checks out each one, looking at herself. Finally, she pulls out a child's doll mirror: oval, the size of a girl's face, trimmed in pink plastic with a handle. She looks at herself, then looks over her shoulder at the audience, she pivots to see the coffee shop, enjoying the view. Mirror Man enters. She sees him and both feel "caught in the act" — he averts his eyes and she quickly puts down the mirror.)

SHELLY. Oh... I didn't see you... Can I get you something? *(Mirror Man moves to his seat with his back to Shelly, showing no response to her.)* I've got some fresh coffee. Do you want cream again? *(She pauses.)* I bet you want your briefcase back. *(Shelly closes up the case.)* It's right up here. We kept it here overnight so it'd be safe. We looked inside for your address. But, there's nothing, you know. *(She pauses.)* OK. Well, it's up here whenever you want it. *(Shelly waits.)* You know, if you don't want coffee or anything, then I can't let you sit there. It's for customers.

MIRROR MAN. *(Without turning.)* Half-and-half with coffee. And sugar. Please.

SHELLY. Sure, no problem. But, you got to pay this time. Coffee's a dollar, and you owe me for yesterday. *(Mirror Man doesn't respond, but retrieves his compact mirror case from his inside coat pocket. He wipes it clean, hesitates, and then raises it over his shoulder to watch*

Shelly through it. With her back to Mirror Man, she fixes his coffee.) Janelle thinks you're a spy or something. From Russia. You're not a spy are you? (*Seeing Mirror Man.*) There you go with that mirror. (*Stalling him.*) Now, you may not know this, but that's not polite in this country. (*She is moving to the counter to retrieve the plastic mirror.*) But, it's a pretty way to see the world, isn't it? Backwards and everything. It's like having your own TV show and you just move that mirror like a camera... to see whatever you want. Right? So, you can sit and look at people and see everything and no one ever sees you. So, right now, I'm on your secret TV show, aren't I...? But, I like TV, too... So, I can just put you on my TV show. (*She pulls out the plastic mirror and begins to watch Mirror Man over her shoulder.*) See? Now, I can watch you. And see right into your eyes. (*Mirror Man flinches. As Shelly moves closer, walking backwards, mirror in hand, Mirror Man cringes. Slowly emphasizing each word.*) I can see right into your eyes. But, you know what's worse? You don't ever see yourself, do you? You watch everybody else, but you don't see yourself. Take a look at yourself... (*Shelly is right upon him. She turns around, flipping her mirror to face him, forcing Mirror Man to see his own eyes through the two mirrors. Mirror Man hides his face and begins sobbing.*)... look right into your heart. (*Shelly pauses, then touches his arm.*) It's ok. It's ok. Being watched changes it, doesn't it? But, I do it — watch something else and hide — you know, we all do... with sunglasses or a TV screen or a nice dress. Everybody watches. And hides. So no one really sees... (*Blackout.*)

* * *

DOWN

by

Janet Kenney

98   THE BOSTON THEATER MARATHON

Down was originally performed at the Second Annual Coyote Theatre Ten Minute Festival in November of 1998. The cast was as follows:

SAM .... John Porrell
BOBBO .... Michael Bradshaw

Down was produced at the First Annual Boston Theater Marathon on April 18th, 1999. Sponsored by Threshold Theatre. Directed by Nathalie Highland. The cast was as follows:

SAM .... Steven Berkheimer
BOBBO .... Deborah Wrighton

For Bud, and for Michael Bradshaw.
Special thanks to Kate Snodgrass.

CHARACTERS

BOBBO — a very, very old man, ill and frail.
SAM — his grandson, about forty.

TIME
Spring, evening.

PLACE
At an old stone bridge that covers a pond.

DOWN

(*Evening insects buzz. Upstage, an old stone bridge with a railing. In front of the bridge, stage left of it, a low stone bench. Beside the bench, a wheelchair. A very old man, Bobbo, and a young man, Sam, stand looking down at the pond. Bobbo is leaning on a three-footed cane. They watch the water, the moon, the sky. Evening insects buzz, birds chirp. The water ripples and splashes under the bridge. Pause. Wheezing.*)

BOBBO. Go get me a beer. Get yourself one too.
SAM. I can't.
BOBBO. I won't tell.
SAM. You don't drink beer.
BOBBO. I know that!
SAM. Well, you just —
BOBBO. You didn't bring any in a cooler? Here. Help me down. (*Sam helps Bobbo to the bench.*) I told you to bring a cooler.
SAM. No sir. You're not supposed —
BOBBO. I know that, ya damn fool.
SAM. I know.
BOBBO. 'Course you know. No beer. That's a shame.
SAM. Yessir. A beer would be nice.
BOBBO. Yeah. Well. Get yourself a beer later.
SAM. Yessir.

BOBBO. You'll need it. It's all right to need a beer once in a while. A beer is a good thing.

SAM. Yessir.

BOBBO. If your liver works. And your kidneys work. And your prostate. Pro-state. Otherwise you're in the john all night, peeing your brains out.

SAM. Right.

BOBBO. Well. You were always a good lawnmower.

SAM. Thank you.

BOBBO. You're welcome.

SAM. But I was not a lawn mower.

BOBBO. Whatsat?

SAM. I was not, personally, a lawn mower.

BOBBO. Mmmm.

SAM. (*Pause.*) Nevermind.

BOBBO. Hmmm.

SAM. It's OK, Bobbo, never —

BOBBO. Oh! Oh! You're not a lawn mower! Oh, not - right, right. Uh-huh, yeah. Not a – yeah —

SAM. You get it.

BOBBO. I do, I do. I get it. Yup. Don't be fresh, Sam.

SAM. Right, Right.

BOBBO. Right.

SAM. Right. I was awake all night. I was praying —

BOBBO. Picked a fine time to start praying, Sam —

SAM. I'm not sure we're right about this. I —

BOBBO. Whattdyamean we're not — not — not right — (*Bobbo starts to cough violently.*)

SAM. OK, OK. You're OK. Settle down. Do you need to go home? Ah, Jesus. All right. Should we — OK. You're all right. All right. Why do you call me Sam?

BOBBO. Sam?

SAM. Yeah, why Sam, instead of —

BOBBO. Oh, oh, that - instead of —
SAM. Instead of my name.
BOBBO. BECAUSE YOU'RE SAM, GODDAMMIT! You've always been Sam! Didn't I always call you Sam?
SAM. Yessir.
BOBBO. I did.
SAM. Right. Yessir. (*Pause. Sam begins to rub Bobbo's stooped back. Pause.*)
SAM. I can feel your ribs through your shirt.
BOBBO. I'm an old man, Sam.
SAM. Yup.
BOBBO. Don't do that, Sam. It doesn't look right. It's a little bit fay.
SAM. Sorry.
BOBBO. I know you mean well. It's nonna my business.
SAM. What?
BOBBO. If you are. You've always been good to me.
SAM. I'm not, Bobbo. I'm not gay. Fay. Not fay.
BOBBO. Oh. Good. That's good. But I'm telling you, you'd still be a good boy.
SAM. I guess.
BOBBO. Get married sometime, will ya, Sam?
SAM. I guess I will. One of these days.
BOBBO. Find the right girl. That's the trick. I wish I could be at your wedding.
SAM. You could —
BOBBO. It's not my fault you waited this long to get married. You're almost forty, for Chrissake —
SAM. Yes, I know —
BOBBO. You know how old you are. You know what I think of you.
SAM. Yeah, I do.

BOBBO. Well.
SAM. What?
BOBBO. I wish you were my boy.
SAM. Yeah. Thanks.
BOBBO. I like you better. I guess it skips a generation.
SAM. I like you better, too.
BOBBO. Your grandmother was a beautiful woman.
SAM. Yes, yes she was.
BOBBO. Keep a picture of her where you can see it.
SAM. All right.
BOBBO. You don't have to keep a picture of me.
SAM. OK.
BOBBO. But don't forget what I looked like —
SAM. No.
BOBBO. Here. Look at me. Look at my face.
SAM. OK —
BOBBO. No, look at it. Look at it, boy.
SAM. I see it. I see it. I can't do it.
BOBBO. Yes, you can.
SAM. No —
BOBBO. Did I not tell you always you could do what you want?
SAM. Yessir.
BOBBO. I always said, you can do what you want. Plus, do what I tell you. Go on now.
SAM. You're not being —
BOBBO. Sam — enough. Enough. Why I need to be tortured like this, I'll never know. If I just trip, say I trip and fall, maybe even fall down a flight of stairs, I'll break a hip. I'll break two hips, I'll linger. Do you want me to linger, Sam?
SAM. No sir.
BOBBO. I'm already lingering, Sam!

SAM. Yessir, I know.

BOBBO. Thank God I never learned to swim! Come on, now, throw me over! I'm light as a feather, boy. You won't even break a sweat! Won't even strain a, strain a muscle, Sam! Come on now, before I change my mind. Go. Go. (*Sam tries, fails.*) Oh, Sam. You disappoint me.

SAM. I'm sorry.

BOBBO. You're not a good boy. Yes you are, yes you are, I'm sorry. I'm sorry. All right. OK. Then, you tried.

SAM. I tried.

BOBBO. You did. You're a good boy. Your grandmother loved you very much.

SAM. Thank you.

BOBBO. Here, here, take it easy. Take it easy. Don't make me buy you an ice cream, Sam. I don't have any money, Sam. You'd have to drive. All right, boy. You were always a good boy. If you have a good grandson, one is enough. That's what we always said. Yeah. One's enough. You were the handsomest boy. You had a set of eyes on you. Lemme see; lemme see. Oh, yeah. You still have 'em. But when your head was smaller, your eyes looked bigger. Your grandmother used to set you on your back and she'd set herself over you and she'd put her face in your face and I couldn't even talk to her then. She didn't care if I was alive or dead or hungry or what, lookin' at you. All right, boy, you did your best. You made your grandmother happy. She used to say you smelled like a baby, and I'd say, of course he smells like a baby, ya damn fool, he is a baby. She loved babies, you know. We shoulda had more kids. Ah, well. Too late now, right? Right? Too late for the old man to breed, eh, Sam?

SAM. You shouldn't do this to me.

BOBBO. Huh? This? This one little favor?

SAM. Favor! It's not a favor. When I was thinking last night, I was hating you.

BOBBO. You don't hate me, Sam.

SAM. No, I don't hate you.

BOBBO. Don't say you hate me.

SAM. I don't. But, come on. What about it? Come on. I promise, one of these days, you won't wake up —

BOBBO. When?

SAM. I don't know —

BOBBO. 'Course you don't know. Could be a year. Could be two years.

SAM. Listen, one of these mornings, they'll call me. And they'll say, Sorry, we're so sorry, you can come and get your —

BOBBO. WHEN???

SAM. I don't know.

BOBBO. See. You don't know when.

SAM. It's a good home —

BOBBO. You wanna live there with me Sam?

SAM. I can't do that —

BOBBO. Oh, sure, all talk.

SAM. I'm not —

BOBBO. I shit my drawers! I shit my drawers, Sam. I wake up and I'm covered. It's the smell, it wakes me up! And the girl comes in, the black girl there, the one I like, what's her name —

SAM. Marie.

BOBBO. Marie. Sam, a man shouldn't do that to himself. He shouldn't do that. And the pain, Sam. Sam, God never intended a man to be in this kind of pain. It's not right.

SAM. I'm sorry. I don't want you to be in pain. I'm just thinking this is not right.

BOBBO. I'm begging you.
SAM. Please.
BOBBO. Please.
SAM. I told Dad. I told him what we were doing.
BOBBO. No you didn't.
SAM. Yes, I did. Maybe I'll end up in jail, I don't know.
BOBBO. Jail. For what?
SAM. For throwing you in the pond! For killing you! It's illegal!
BOBBO. You're not killing me! Marie is killing me. "Oh, there we go, all nice and clean. You smell like a bed of roses, Mr. J. You're a shinin' beauty, you are, Mr. J. Nice and clean." Marie is killing me.
SAM. I can ask her to stop saying that.
BOBBO. Leave her alone. She doesn't know what else to say.
SAM. I didn't tell Dad.
BOBBO. I know. So no one knows.
SAM. It'll look suspicious, taking you to our pond for the day.
BOBBO. No it won't.
SAM. It will.
BOBBO. It's poetry. A man should die where he was happy. Should be his wife. Should be his wife at his side.
SAM. Should be his wife tossing him into the pond.
BOBBO. Don't be fresh, Sam. (*Bobbo gets himself up. He walks over to the bridge.*)
SAM. Should I?
BOBBO. You know, one good grandson, that's all you need.
SAM. Yessir. (*Sam picks up the old man; he cradles him.*) Jesus. You don't weigh a thing.

* * *

FRANCE

by

Bill Lattanzi

France was workshopped in the Manhattan Punch Line Festival of One-act Comedies, in March 1990. The play premiered in September, 1997 at NewGate Theater, Providence, Rhode Island. It was directed by Vera Wayne. The cast was as follows:

M.T. CASE . . . . Bruce Newbury
M. PASTEUR . . . . Laurent Y. Andruet

France was produced at the First Annual Boston Theater Marathon on April 18th, 1999. Sponsored by Rough & Tumble Theatre. Directed by Dan Milstein. The cast was as follows:

M.T. CASE . . . . Jon Blackstone
M. PASTEUR . . . . Gregory Bouchard
THE FRENCH . . . . . . Kristin Baker, Helen McElwain,
John Rahal Sarrouf, Joe Wex.

for Antoine Doinel

CHARACTERS

PASTEUR — French
CASE — American
THE FRENCH — The people of France

TIME
The Present.

PLACE
A small office in the United States.

FRANCE

(An office. Pasteur at a desk. Enter Case.)

CASE. Yes, I'd like to apply...
PASTEUR. Bonjour!
CASE. Yes, I'd like to apply -
PASTEUR. Bonjour, I say!
CASE. Yes. Bonjour. I'd like to apply — *(Pasteur is dumbstruck at Case's pronunciation. He tries to help.)*
PASTEUR. Non, non, non. .....Bon – jour.
CASE. Bon-jour.
PASTEUR. Bonjour.
CASE. Bonjour.
PASTEUR. *(Extremely slowly.)* Bon. ....
CASE. *(Ever the good student.)* Bon. ....
PASTEUR. ....Jour. ....
CASE. ....Jour. ....
PASTEUR. BONJOUR!!
CASE. Bonjour. *(A beat.)* Yes, I'd like to apply -
PASTEUR. How did you hear of us?
CASE. I'd like. ... In the newspaper. Under France.
PASTEUR. Yes, yes, fine, here, France is the place. You are in the right location, proximally. Allow me to introduce myself. *(Case waits.)* Allow me to introduce myself... *(Case waits some more.)* ALLOW me to introduce myself.
CASE. Oh. Yes. Go right ahead.

PASTEUR. Thank you. I am Pasteur. Charmed.
CASE. Ah. Pasteur. I enjoy your milk.
PASTEUR. (*Incensed.*) Pasteur does not appreciate this joke. It is not French.
CASE. I'm sorry. (*Pasteur does paperwork.*) I'd like to apply to...
PASTEUR. Name.
CASE. ...For the position you advertised of...
PASTEUR. NAME, s'il vous plait.
CASE. Case.
PASTEUR. Case of...? Casse de what?
CASE. Case. Case of nothing. M. T. Case. M.T., for nothing. Empty, get it? My parents had a sense of humor.
PASTEUR. Worse than yours. Not French at all. What is it, Mister Nothing?
CASE. Case, Mister Case, if you please.
PASTEUR. Case of nothing, Case. Never born Mister Nothing? Mister American Nothing?
CASE. I'd like to apply for the advertised position of -
PASTEUR. You'd like to apply to go to France?
CASE. Go to France? Go to France. Well, I imagine that would be part of it. Travel. The advertisement didn't say that travel would be involved, but, well, travel is good. Broadens the mind. Broadens our outlook. Our horizons. And travel would be fine by me. (*Pasteur is waiting...*)
PASTEUR. You would like to go to France, oui ou non?
CASE. Yes.
PASTEUR. (*Wags his finger.*) Unh, unh, unh —
CASE. Oui.
PASTEUR. Bon. Allors. Good. Maintenant. Now. You would like to go to France.
CASE. Oui.
PASTEUR. (*Wags his finger again.*) Unh, unh, unh —

CASE. Yes.

PASTEUR. Parfait. Bon. Allors. Maintenant. Cookie, baby, sweetie, honey, my homes — You would like to go to France now?

CASE. Oui. Yes. Oui. I certainly — now?

PASTEUR. Bien Sur! Of course. (*They go to France.*)

CASE. Wow. It's beautiful.

PASTEUR. Oui.

CASE. Oui. It's even more beautiful than I —

PASTEUR. And now we return.

CASE. Return? But we just... (*They return.*)... got here. There. How did you...

PASTEUR. That will be five thousand francs.

CASE. Five thousand francs? But I'm here to apply for —

PASTEUR. Payable in cash. American dollars. A credit card is fine. As you prefer.

CASE. You're supposed to pay me. I came to apply for a job —

PASTEUR. Merci beaucoup, you may pay outside. Thank you.

CASE. Now, see here, my very good man...

PASTEUR. You have a complaint?

CASE. Yes, I have a complaint. If you think that I'm going to sit here, while you and your miserable firm —

PASTEUR. I am exactly correct.

CASE. Oh, you think so.

PASTEUR. Monsieur Case, I ask you. Did you not experience the varied wonders and ancient glories of La Belle France? Did you not ogle the women and devour the food? Devour the women and ogle the food? Did you not admire Le Métro? Did you not complain of the snootiness? Did you not despair of the language? You did not? It is not my fault. Ce n'est pas ma faute. Oui? Non? Bon. Allors. These things cannot be helped. If you did no, you did not. It is of little consequence what actually occurred, Monsieur Case. Don't you remember? Why, I recall your very words: "Wow. It's beautiful." I have saved you time, Monsieur Case. I have given you the exact experience which you desired at a loss of almost no time. time is money, Monsieur Case. L'argent! Five thousand francs. Very worthwhile. Thank you. All of the above. Vive La France!

>   (*Sings La Marseillaise. Music, perhaps Piaf. The stage fills with French men and women in various types: a painter, a De Gaulle, a Piaf, a Bardot, a Godard, a Napoleon, Josephine Baker. A line of Can-Can girls sing and dance. A stripe-shirted sailor fights with a knife-wielding whore. A mime performs. A kindly balloonnier sells balloons. They sing. They hold sparklers. The Tri-Color unfurls. The stage is full of life.*)

Boeuf Bourguignon! Le Jazz Hot! La Rive Gauche! Le Côte D'Azur. L'Age D'Or. Les Boules-de-neige! This is a ball of snow, but it is far too beautiful a thing to say, "ball of snow," and so, you see, we say... Boules-de-Neige! Les Folies Bergères...!.. Apollinaire! Henri Toulouse-Lautrec! Giscard D'Estange! Manet, Monet, Massenet, Miou-Miou ...
    CASE. Pasteur. (*Everything stops.*)
    PASTEUR. Oui? Monsieur Case of Nothing? Monsieur Zero?
    CASE. Please, please, Pasteur.
    PASTEUR. Oui?

CASE. (*Throughout the following speech Case develops a French accent. He takes off his tie, his jacket, rips his shirt open.*) Pasteur, I'll pay. I'll pay anything you want. I want more. More, more and more of France. I want to stroll down the Champs-Elysees. I want to linger in an uncrowded cafe. I don't want to shower so much anymore. Clean, clean, all the time clean, what is this obsession with clean?!! I want to take a mistress! I want to sit through very difficult films with no car chases, and nod "Oui. Oui. C'est la vie, c'est la guerre." I'm tired of being this American blob, this mutt of many nations. Yes, I want to be French. French, French, everything French! Every fiber, every sinew, tout à fait, I want to be French. I want to believe deep in my soul that there lives un génie du film extraordinaire qui s'appelle Jerry Lewis! Pasteur!

(*Singing resumes. Cannons blast. Pasteur sits back down at his desk. The crowd of French surround Case to create a magic circle. As he speaks, they may touch him, muss his hair, remove clothing, in general prepare him for some unknowable ritual.*)

Jean-Pierre Leaud! Jean-Louis Barrault! Jean-Paul Sartre! À la carte! Jean-Luc Godard, Fragonard! Jean-Jacque Rousseau, Jean-Jacque Annoux. Jacque Chirac! Jeanne d'arc. Jean Naté , Ile de la Cite! France Gall! Claude Charbrol! Eugene Atget! Etienne Aigner! Jeanne Moreau, François Truffaut, Antoine Doinel, Antoine Doinel, Antoine Doinel... Pompidou! Depardieu! Luc Besson! Robert Bresson! La Rive Gauche...! Juliette Binoche!!! Bardot! Bordeaux! Q'est-ce que c'est? Beaujolais! Diderot, Derrida, Didier!!! Oui!! Oui!!! J'avoir besoins d'etre Francais!!!

(Case suffers a massive coronary attack and pitches forward, suddenly dead. The music finishes. The French drift off, disinterested. Calm returns.)

PASTEUR. *(With a shrug.)* For some, to be French, is rich for the blood. Next Case, s'il vous plait! *(Blackout.)*

* * *

THE LESSON

by

Melinda Lopez

The Lesson premiered at the First Annual Boston Theater Marathon on April 18th, 1999. Sponsored by Shakespeare & Company. Directed by Tina Packer & Michael Hammond. The cast was as follows:
CARPENTER .... Anne-Marie Cusson

CHARACTERS

Carpenter

TIME — Lunch time.

PLACE — A building site.

THE LESSON

(Woman carpenter, forty. She wears a tool belt, hard hat. House frame stands behind her. She is seated on a sawhorse eating a sandwich. House frame stands behind her.)

WOMAN. Just working with a hammer, how hard is that? Driving nails into a board. Twelve penny nails. But the kid is just pounding away like he wants to massacre that board, like he's got a personal grudge against it. I say, "Hold on son, you don't have to beat it to death, you just ease that nail in. Make like your just easin' that nail in." And I give him the hammer. Bam blam blam, he goes poundin, wackin the board, missing the nail altogether — I'm telling you that two by four, I thought for sure it would just crack into ten pieces. The kid's eleven, but the kid is strong. "Why are you massacring that wood? Just tease it in, make like that board is your friend, and you're just gonna tease the nail in. A little gentleness goes a long way." And I show him again, and he turns to me and says, in the dirtiest way I ever heard, "That's the *girl* way. I'm not pounding any nails like some *girl*."

And I'll tell you, he said that word like it was the dirtiest word he knew. And I'll tell you, and I'm not proud of this, but I just lost my temper. I did. I lost my temper and I —

kind of unconscious-like I guess, I put that hammer into my left hand, thank the Lord I did that, and I just hauled off and I belted him hard with my right. I hit him. Smacked him right in the middle of his face. I'm not proud of it, but I'll tell you just his tone, his tone of voice made my blood freeze up, and kind of unconscious-like, I placed that hammer in my left hand, and belted him with my right, like it was the most natural thing in the world. And he's all bawling and screaming, and his lip is bleeding, and I'll tell you, I did not feel badly. No I did not. And I said to him, "That there's a girls upper cut. And there ain't no difference between that upper cut and a man's upper cut."

And that little snot nosed kid, well he runs off and gets his papa, all wailing and screaming that I'd broken his nose — and it is true, I'm not saying that it ain't true, but what I am saying is that I have never heard a boy crying like that. It shocked me. Honest it did. Don't seem natural a boy crying like that. And he runs off and gets his papa.

Now Stanley, he sees the blood on that boy's face and hears him screeching like a banshee, and comes running out of the house hell bent for leather, saying, "Who done this, I'll kill em..." And that little brat standing there he says, "It was your *girl* friend, that *girl* over there." And I hear that same tone, that same nasty, nasty tone in his piggy little mouth, and it's all I can do, I swear it's all I can do to keep from hauling off with my left. And Stanley's there, a little dumb now, just looking at me with his mouth hanging open, and then he says, finally, "Well Jaysus, Anne Marie, what'd you go and do that for? He's just a kid."

And in that second, I could really see, just see how they

THE LESSON 119

start, how they, you know how they trap us into it. It starts with one dirty look, one little sneer and we just let it go by — one whistle, one tuna fish joke. And we say, he didn't mean it, he's just a boy. And then that boy, he grow and grow, and soon that boy, he starts to pinching and brushing up against you, like you weren't nothin in the world, and sitting too close and spitting in your ear and wrestling off your prom dress and marrying you and ruining your life. And all them other boys learning the same from him.

And so I drew my line in the sand, in a manner of speakin, and I said, "Look here Stanley, you a good, hard-working man, and I like you. We been dating for five weeks now, and I ain't never been nothing but real honest with you. You asked me to teach your son something today. You know I don't have a maternal bone in my body as it were. You know that's why my first two husbands left me. You know damn well, I am the best carpenter in all of Peach Tree county, and I'll be good goddamned if I'm going to have some snot-nose-tadpole calling me a girl to my face. Now if this child of yours wants to learn to drive a nail in my way, then he can keep his mouth to hisself. But if he don't, then I'll send him flying clear over to the Arkansas border every time he gets in my face. He ain't no kid. And he ain't too young to learn a thing or two about women."

And Stanley got real quiet, and that boy, he standing there sniffling and bleeding, and after a might long pause, Stan he says, "Well then, I'd say that there's enough learning for a Sunday afternoon. What's say we go to the DQ for double dip?" And that boy, he starts laughing, and jumping up and down, and the blood mixing with the snot and the tears, and him smiling away. And he turns to me, just like nothing ever happened between us, and he says, "Auntie Marie, can we take the Harley?" (*She checks her watch, begins packing up her lunch.*) One o'clock, straight up. If they see me loafin, they take liberties. (*Calls to crew offstage.*) All right men, back to work, let's see some hustle. Clear out that AC plywood, plumber needs access later today. And don't use those studs. Twisted as a cheese doodle — what con- artist is selling those? Stanley, haul your ass into town and get me some decent lumber. My name is on this house. (*Lights fade.*)

* * *

SHOTGUN WEDDING

by

Renita Martin

Shotgun Wedding premiered at the First Annual Boston Theater Marathon on April 18th, 1999. Produced by African Repertory Troupe. Directed by Cassandra M. Cato-Louis. Costumes by Dale Patterson. The cast was as follows:

FATHER .... Michael Nurse
MOTHER .... Yasmin Dixon
ALBERT .... Shaun Taylor
APRIL .... C.M. Cato-Louis
CHILDREN .... Chanti Parker,
J. Layla Louis, Natasha Brown

to my grandfather and grandmother — the Griffins.

CHARACTERS

FATHER
MOTHER
ALBERT
APRIL
CHILDREN

SHOTGUN WEDDING

(Lights rise on the inside of the front door of a modest country house. A Mother opens the door. Albert, a young man in his late teens, enters. He is draped in guilt and fear. Mother and Albert exit upstage right.

Two Little Girls who have peeked this scene from around the corner run into the bedroom of April, the oldest daughter.

Lights rise on April's bed. She has a pillow over her head. The Two Little Girls snatch the pillow, stand her up, and help her get ready to go into the living room. April is pregnant and showing.

Lights up on the living room. April and Albert sit stiffly on the couch. They are almost at opposite ends of the couch. Mother and Father sit in chairs directly across from them. Father is cleaning his gun. His routine — cleaning. Spitting on trouble spots. Blowing. Pointing. Putting parts back together — should be deliberate. Albert should build a rhythm with Father — Albert should cross and uncross his legs, adjust his collar... The underbeat should be April and Albert moving closer to one another from opposite ends of the couch. This rhythm should crescendo with Albert placing money on the table.

Everything should stop, the children should look at one another as if the apocalypse has arrived. April should be profoundly insulted and cry. And Father should be finished cleaning his gun and just about to take aim. At the height of tension, Albert snatches the money from the table, reaches inside his jacket on the other side, gets on one knee, and hands April an wedding ring.

Mother and April hug, Mother runs to hug Albert, who looks like someone just snatched away the rug that was his life. April runs to hug Father. Father slowly gets up, and puts the gun down. Lights fade.)

* * *

ORAL REPORT

by

Jack Neary

Oral Report premiered at the First Annual Boston Theater Marathon on April 18th, 1999. Sponsored by New Repertory Theatre. Directed by Adam Zahler. The cast was as follows:

GERT .... Kate Carney
ALMA .... Patricia Till
MARJORIE .... Alice Duffy

CHARACTERS

GERT — direct, opinionated.
ALMA — losing her hearing, and has evolved through life assimilating only the basic information necessary to make it to her late seventies.
MARJORIE — quiet, intelligent, circumspect, careful.

ORAL REPORT

(Three women in their seventies sit on Alma's porch in a blue collar neighborhood of eastern Massachusetts. Each lady has her own sense of humor, even irony, though none of them would acknowledge that irony has anything to do with anything. It is a balmy summer evening, and the women relax in what appears to be a nightly ritual — sitting and gabbing and catching up on neighborhood activities.

As the curtain rises, we find the women staring out at whatever it is that's in front of their eyes. Silence, for a moment. Finally, Gert contributes.)

GERT. He can't park there, you know.
ALMA. What?
GERT. He can't park there.
ALMA. Who?
GERT. Him. There. With the car. Sister Bernadetta'll be outa the convent before he gets outa the car. You watch. She don't want anybody parkin' in the school parkin' lot. Since they got the new lines drawn and all the new spaces so it's easy to park, she don't want anybody parkin' there.
ALMA. Why not?
GERT. It's like all her life she's been waitin' for her own parkin' lot or somethin'. She's 12, her mother says whatdya

wanna be, she says a nun or a parking lot attendant. She's like Mussolini with the parkin' lot. Look. Here she comes. (*Beat, as they watch.*) Look at 'im. "Yes, Sister. Yes, Sister. Sorry, Sister." You'd think she was carryin' a gun.

ALMA. She has a gun?

GERT. (*Loud; directly to Alma.*) No. You'd think she was.

ALMA. Who?

GERT. Bernadetta.

ALMA. (*Long beat, to Marjorie.*) I didn't see a gun. Did you?

MARJORIE. (*Loud, so Alma gets the point.*) It was a joke, Alma. Gert told you a joke.

ALMA. Oh. (*Beat.*) I guess I don't get it.

GERT. (*Looks to parking lot.*) There he goes.

ALMA. (*Longer beat; then, to Gert.*) What's his name? Mussolini?

GERT. Never mind about Mussolini. (*To Marjorie.*) So did you see 'im?

ALMA. Who?

GERT. On the T.V.

MARJORIE. I saw him.

ALMA. Who?

GERT. Lookin' in the camera as if he's talkin' right to me, sayin' them things to me like he knows me.

ALMA. Who?

GERT. His nibs! In Washington.

MARJORIE. The President.

GERT. Thinks I don't know he's full of it.

ALMA. The President?

MARJORIE. He's a politician.

ALMA. They say he mighta did it with... uh...

GERT. Oh, he did it, all right.

ALMA. Uh... that girl. The fat girl. With the funny hat.

MARJORIE. But the people still like him.

ALMA. It was on the T.V.

MARJORIE. The polls. They like him.

ALMA. The Polacks like him?

GERT. I'll tell you who likes him. The people who do what he done like him because they done it too and they wanna keep doin' it and it makes 'em feel better to know he done it and he's gonna get away with it.

MARJORIE. He just might.

GERT. And those of us who only do it when we're supposed to do it, nobody asks us what we think.

MARJORIE. I wonder why.

GERT. Because them that take the polls wanna keep doin' it too. It's one of them conspiracies.

ALMA. He says he didn't do it.

GERT. Oh, he did it.

ALMA. He said it on the T.V. "I did not have sexual... relations with that woman... Miss..." whatever her name is... the Polish girl. Maybe that's why they like him.

GERT. That's what he thinks, you know.

MARJORIE. Well...

GERT. He thinks what he done isn't sexual relations.

ALMA. Wait a minute...

GERT. He thinks we're dumb enough to believe that what he done isn't sexual relations in the legal sense.

ALMA. Wait a minute. Did he or didn't he?

GERT. What?

ALMA. Do it.

GERT. Oh, he did it.

MARJORIE. Depends on what you mean, Alma.

ALMA. What depends?

MARJORIE. Well, the President thinks... or at least he says he thinks... that what he did... with the girl... wasn't sexual relations.

ALMA. Well what was it he did?

MARJORIE. He... wasn't clear on that.

ALMA. He didn't know?

MARJORIE. Well...

ALMA. How can he not know what it is? He's the President, isn't he?

MARJORIE. It's not that he doesn't know what it is. He just thinks... that the way he... did it, doesn't... add up to... what he calls... sexual relations.

ALMA. (*Beat.*) The way he did it?

MARJORIE. Yes.

ALMA. The way he did it don't add up?

MARJORIE. Not to him.

ALMA. (*Beat.*) Well, once you do it, you know you did it, don't you?

GERT. It's the way he done it makes him say it isn't relations.

ALMA. What way did he do it?

MARJORIE. Well, I can't...

ALMA. What way?

MARJORIE. I really don't want to...

ALMA. What way did he do it?

GERT. He did the oral.

ALMA. The oral?

GERT. He says for it to be sexual relations you have to have it with intercourse. (*Beat, to the inquiring Alma.*) With the genitals on the genitals.

ALMA. With the what on the what?

GERT. The genitals on the genitals. He says it isn't sexual relations if it's oral sex.

ALMA. What kind of sex?
GERT. Oral.
ALMA. Oral?
GERT. Oral. You know what oral means, don't you?
ALMA. Out loud?
GERT. No. Oral. Oral. With the mouth.
ALMA. (*Beat.*) What, he talks while he's doin' it?
GERT. Let's put it this way, when he's gettin' it done, if anybody's doin' any talkin', it's him.
ALMA. (*To Marjorie.*) What's she talkin' about?
MARJORIE. It's a different kind of sex, Alma. Not the way we used to do it.
GERT. Don't tell me you never heard of oral sex?
ALMA. I never heard of sex at all till after my fourth kid. We didn't call it anything, we just went at it. By that time I only knew one way and it worked, so we didn't do it any more ways. (*Beat.*) Once he let me be on top so he could see the Super Bowl. So what is it? Oral sex.
GERT. (*To Marjorie.*) Tell her.
MARJORIE. I'm not telling her.
ALMA. (*To Marjorie.*) Did you ever do it?
MARJORIE. Oh, no.
ALMA. (*To Gert.*) Did you?
GERT. I thought about it. I asked the priest in confession once if I could. He said he'd get back to me. Nobody ever asked him before, he said. Two days later he gets transferred to Africa. So I never tried it.
ALMA. So what is it?
GERT. Figure it out. Oral. Oral. The mouth.
ALMA. Yeah, so what?
GERT. Oral. The mouth. Sex. Sex. Oral sex.
ALMA. (*Beat.*) Kissin'?
GERT. Not kissin'. Kissin' involves two noses in the

same general vicinity. With the oral, you got your noses in two different counties.

ALMA. What are we talkin' about here, nose sex?

GERT. No. We're talkin' about the vicinities where the various noses end up when the sex is happening.

ALMA. *(Beat.)* What?

GERT. Look, what's the nearest thing to your nose on your face?

ALMA. My little mustache thingy.

GERT. That you kiss with! The nearest thing to your nose on your face that you kiss with.

ALMA. Lips?

GERT. Lips. So with the oral you follow your nose and that's where the lips end up. Yours and his. In different places.

ALMA. What places?

GERT. Well... she goes down there...

MARJORIE. Good Lord...

ALMA. Down where?

GERT. There. There. The sexual area.

ALMA. His sexual area?

GERT. She goes down there and she... she... services him.

ALMA. So wait a minute, if she's down there... in his sexual area... with her nose...

GERT. Yes?

ALMA. Don't that mean her own sexual area is way off the target?

GERT. This time, her nose is her general sexual area.

MARJORIE. Jesus, Mary and Joseph.

ALMA. She's not... She's not...

GERT. Oh, yes, she is.

ALMA. Her nose... and his... thing?

ORAL REPORT 133

GERT. Forget about the nose, Alma! Expand your horizons!

ALMA. Lips?

GERT. Lips.

ALMA. (*Major disbelief.*) Go on!

GERT. Oral. Mouth. Sex. Sex. Oral sex.

ALMA. (*Beat.*) What'll they think of next? (*To Marjorie.*) You knew about this?

MARJORIE. I read about it.

ALMA. (*To Gert.*) How did you find out?

GERT. I get a pay per view every once in a while.

ALMA. (*Long beat.*) Then what happens?

GERT. To what?

ALMA. When she starts nosin' around down there, what happens then?

GERT. Well, that's when you get into personal preference.

MARJORIE. Oh, I think they took care of personal preference about the time she put her nose into his sexual area.

GERT. Well, I mean once she's there, you know, with his whodjie in her... whatever... then it's up to them, you know, to decide how far they want to go.

ALMA. You're not tellin' me...

GERT. I'm not tellin' you anything except that if you're on the receivin' end of that particular main course, you better decide pretty quick whether you want dessert or not.

MARJORIE. (*Disgusted.*) Oh, Gert...

GERT. I'm just sayin'...

ALMA. Dessert?

MARJORIE. (*To Gert.*) Don't look at me.

GERT. So, you can imagine. Either you want to deal with it or you don't. If you don't, you gotta be very agile with your neck.

ALMA. (*Long beat.*) So that's what he was doin' with the Polish girl out in the hallway.

GERT. Seems to be. He just don't think it counted as relations, though. I think he needs a good boot in the ass.

MARJORIE. (*Beat.*) He'd probably enjoy it.

GERT. Look! She got another one!

MARJORIE. Why doesn't she just put up a couple of those orange cones, block off the entrance?

GERT. She likes catchin' them too much. It's a nun thing. The only way she'd be happier is if she could hit them with a fifty cent fine.

ALMA. (*Long beat, as they stare.*) Oral sex.

MARJORIE. Times have changed, Alma.

ALMA. (*Beat.*) Oral. Mouth. Sex. Sex. Oral sex.

GERT. We should send Bernadetta to Washington. He wouldn't pull any of that stuff with her. Or at least she'd hit him for more than fifty cents. (*Chuckles.*)

MARJORIE. Oh, Gert...

ALMA. (*The longest beat.*) I won't sleep for a month.

* * *

PEAS

by

Aidan Parkinson

Peas premiered at the First Annual Boston Theater Marathon on April 18th, 1999. Sponsored by Fire Dog Theatre, Inc. Directed by Daniel Kramer. The cast was as follows:

YOUNG MAN .... Ciaran Crawford
OLD MAN .... Michael Bradshaw

CHARACTERS

OLD MAN
YOUNG MAN

TIME

The present

PLACE

Dublin, Ireland

PEAS

(In a pool of light an Old Man sits weakly, precariously, at a small, red, formica-topped table with chipped, rusting, tubular legs. Two chairs with torn, red, plastic coverings. Old Man in dirty white shirt, dark suspenders, dark trousers and ancient, red slippers. He stares straight ahead. Off, we hear the Young Man moving around a kitchen. When he enters, he is wearing half-mast trousers, red suspenders, polished Doc Martin boots and an immaculate, white shirt.)

YOUNG MAN. *(Off.)* D'ye want peas? *(No response from Old Man who continues to stare, weak, wan and struggling to breathe.)*

YOUNG MAN. *(Entering. Loudly.)* I said, d'ye want peas.

OLD MAN. *(Laboured intake of breath.)* Where's yer mother gone?

YOUNG MAN. Are ye worried?

OLD MAN. She knows not to leave me alone with you.

YOUNG MAN. Maybe she's decided she wants ye dead too. *(A beat. Loudly.)* D'ye want peas?

OLD MAN. I won't eat an'thin' you gimme.

YOUNG MAN. Suit yerself. It's not everyday I cook. *(Exit to kitchen. The old man tries to stand, succeeds, just about, looks around, frightened, considering a way out.*

A beat. Falls back into chair. Pause.)

OLD MAN. I need to pee.

YOUNG MAN. (*Off.*) Just pee yer pants like ye always do.

OLD MAN. I don't want to pee me pants today.

YOUNG MAN. (*Entering with plate of food, mashed potatoes, peas, ground beef, which he slides carelessly onto the table.*) An' why not today? Are ye goin' on a date? Sex, is that it? There's a ride in the works?!

OLD MAN. I haven't peed me pants in two days. I'd like to keep them dry.

YOUNG MAN. I'm not carryin' ye up them stairs, ye smelly fuck! The last time I did that the fumes nearly killed me.

OLD MAN. I don't smell today.

YOUNG MAN. Like fuck ye don't.

OLD MAN. Don't talk to me like that.

YOUNG MAN. Like what?

OLD MAN. 'Smelly fuck.'

YOUNG MAN. Ye are a smelly fuck. An' if ye died this minute ye'd be doin' us all a favor. (*A beat.*) Includin' yerself maybe.

OLD MAN. I'm peein'.

YOUNG MAN. Aw, Jesus Christ!

OLD MAN. I told ye.

YOUNG MAN. Ye told me ye didn't want to pee yer pants today.

OLD MAN. It's awful. I hate it.

YOUNG MAN. What?

OLD MAN. This... bein' like this.

YOUNG MAN. I wish I had some fuckin' poison or somethin'. Some rat shit, or weed or chemical or somethin'.

OLD MAN. Why?

YOUNG MAN. (*Laughing.*) Why, he says? Why? Jesus! (*Exasperated.*) Eat yer dinner. (*The Old Man, bent over, stares into his dinner in disgust. He maneuvers a little in discomfort because of his wet trousers.*)

OLD MAN. Me legs isn't workin' anymore.

YOUNG MAN. It's more than yer legs isn't workin'. Yer pisser isn't workin' an' yer brain's not far behind. Sooner the better. Save yerself a lot o' trouble.

OLD MAN. What?

YOUNG MAN. Look, will I just hit ye over the head with a fryin' pan or somethin'? Push ye down the stairs or cut yer wrists in the bath an' make it look like suicide? (*Pause.*)

OLD MAN. I don't want to die.

YOUNG MAN. Well, that's hard luck, coz the wind's about to blow ye away any minute now. Your time has come old man, an' all I'm sayin' is...

OLD MAN. I'm gonna do a shit.

YOUNG MAN. Aw, for fucksake!

OLD MAN. Take me to the toilet. (*The Young Man looks at him in disgust. The Old Man groans a little in pain, his bowels not quite working properly either. Perhaps a fart. The Young Man, thinking he has no option, goes to lift the Old Man, but withdraws instantly with the stench of the urine and the fart, coughing.*)

YOUNG MAN. I can't. Honestly. I can't take it... Jesus Christ, me eyes are waterin' with the fumes. (*Pause.*) Will I ring the doctor?

OLD MAN. For what?

YOUNG MAN. I dunno. Ye're lookin' pretty bad to me.

OLD MAN. I'm dyin'.

YOUNG MAN. No such fuckin' luck! You've been dyin' for the last five years, an' every day everyone around ye wishes ye dead, wishes ye'd just give us all a break, but no, on ye go regardless. It's like ye want to torture us, it's like ye want to make it hell for yer family so's we'll never forget ye.

OLD MAN. An' me?

YOUNG MAN. An' you wha'?

OLD MAN. I'm bein' tortured. Me legs isn't workin'.

YOUNG MAN. Fuck yer legs! Jesus, I can barely bear the sight o' ye.

(The Old Man stares. A couple of beats, then he falls into his dinner, face first. The Young Man looks at him. Waits. Looks some more. Approaches him apprehensively. The Old Man is deathly still. The Young Man raises the Old Man's head by the hair. There is food stuck to his face: potato in his eyes, a few peas embedded in the potatoes. He looks dead. The Young Man lets the Old Man's head fall back into the dinner, hoots for joy, exits to kitchen, and reenters almost immediately with a cordless telephone. On phone.)

I think he's gone... No, I didn't call the doctor... He just fell into his dinner... Look, you just come home an' see for yerself... *(Phone off. The Old Man stirs.)* Oh, fuck! *(Enraged, then hopeless.)* If you don't die, old man, I'll... Jesus... I'll... Fuck, what the hell am I goin' to do with ye?! Ye'll destroy us all, ye will! Ye'll wear us all out! What the hell are we goin' to do?!

OLD MAN. *(Lifts his head. Licks food off his lips.)* Nice peas. I've always had a thing for sweet garden peas. *(Lights down.)*

* * *

VIRGIN TERRITORY

by

Payne Ratner

Virgin Territory premiered at the First Annual Boston Theater Marathon on April 18th, 1999. Sponsored by Súgán Theatre Company. Directed by Donna Sorbello. The cast was as follows:

DARWIN .... Jonathan Bradshaw
MONTY .... Alex Wallace
WOMAN .... Rena Baskin

To my wife Renee and my son Graham.

CHARACTERS

MONTY — Overweight. 15 years old.
DARWIN — Monty's one, tenuous friend.

PLACE
An old, inexpensive motel room.

TIME
The present.

VIRGIN TERRITORY

(*Lights up. Monty sits on the foot of a cheap, motel room bed. He's wearing only white briefs and black socks. He's staring at the T.V. which is off. There is the sound of water running and a woman singing in the shower.*)

MONTY. I didn't know she sang so good. (*He gets up, looks in mirror. He sucks his belly in. Pulls his underwear up, tries to hold it. His belly flops down. He gets his tee shirt, puts it on, sits back down as before. He suddenly stands up, takes off tee shirt, throws it on chair. His leg is jiggling nervously.*) Mamma Mia, Mamma Mia. (*He blows on his palms. Then he delivers this very monotonously.*) First you gotta warm 'em up with foreplay. They love foreplay. Foreplay is teasing. Foreplay is when you put your hands in your underpants and say, 'Mine, you can't have it'. They love that. That takes about a minute, depending on the girl. Then you jump into bed and say, my hot dog's gonna make you a real woman. That gets 'em crazy. Then you lick their chin and whine like a miniature poodle. They try to push you away and that's a sign they want it more. It drives 'em nuts. Lick and whine, lick and whine. They claw up your back up, rip out your spine, roto-till your scalp... it's fantastic. (*A beat.*) Oh baby baby baby baby baby. (*A beat.*) They like it when you say Oh baby baby baby. The louder the better. If you scream, like, twenty thousand decibels they cum all at once. The vibrations do it. You say oh, baby baby you got me where it counts. Squeeze hard. They like that. Impersonations are good. And they like it when you scream you're cumming and then you jump up on the bed and bounce around with your pecker standing out about a mile and you yell, I ain't had it so good since Nam! They love that. It drives them crazy. (*Pause.*) That's what my brother says. (*Pause.*) He says if you can stand up on the dresser and bend way over and show them your moon. They really like that —

DARWIN. (*From under bed.*) Monty?

MONTY. What?

DARWIN. I gotta whiz. (*Darwin crawls out from under bed.*)

MONTY. Hey. Get back under the bed!

DARWIN. How long she gonna be in there?

MONTY. You can't pee now!

DARWIN. I can't hold it!

MONTY. Oh, Darwin! Please!

DARWIN. Go look and see if the shower curtain's dark.

MONTY. You're gonna pee with her in the shower?! Standing right next to her?!

DARWIN. What's she gonna know if it's me or — ?

MONTY. She'd know it's not me. My brother says I got a very weird smell.

DARWIN. You can get an infection, holding it back.

MONTY. Go out there in the courtyard.

DARWIN. That's not a courtyard, that's a tree.

MONTY. Go behind the tree.

DARWIN. One tree. One tree with stupid old people sitting all around it. Staring at it.

MONTY. They like to watch it growing, Darwin. It's

the only live thing in three blocks. You can't blame 'em.
DARWIN. Wait. Wait.
MONTY. What?
DARWIN. It went away. I don't have to anymore. (*He kneels as if to climb back under bed.*) Now I do. (*He stands up.*) Now I don't. (*A beat.*) It's something about being down there...
MONTY. Oh, Darwin, please. (*He listens at door.*) I don't know how long they take showers.
DARWIN. It's the gurgling water. The sound comes out under the door and goes along the floor. Up here there's other sounds. Maybe if I stand real still over there by curtains —
MONTY. My brother says they don't like knowing there's someone in the room till right afterwards.
DARWIN. Well how fast can you do it?
MONTY. My brother says the faster the better is how they like it.
DARWIN. Just make sure you leave on the light.
MONTY. Why?
DARWIN. 'Cause the flash thing doesn't work.
MONTY. Oh, Darwin!
DARWIN. I borrowed the camera. How was I supposed to know the flash thing didn't —
MONTY. She said on one condition... that I didn't have the light on.
DARWIN. Why?
MONTY. She's embarrassed 'cause of her face.
DARWIN. You want the picture or not?
MONTY. Yes. I have to have the picture.
DARWIN. So, when she's ripping out your spine just reach out and turn on the light and I'll come out. (*A beat.*)
MONTY. I thought maybe you can get it so her face

doesn't show.

DARWIN. How's your brother gonna know it's her?

MONTY. Yeah. (*Pause.*)

DARWIN. You shoulda asked Sara Carlsbad to do it. Sara Carlsbad would say cheese.

MONTY. This is best, Darwin. My brother said anybody could do it with Sara Carlsbad. (*A beat.*) Listen. Can you hear that? How she sings? Did you ever think a song like that could come out of her?

DARWIN. I figured she howled at the moon.

MONTY. My brother said no man alive would touch her with a ten foot pole.

DARWIN. You'll go where no man has gone before.

MONTY. I have to have that picture, Darwin. I have to.

DARWIN. Now it's coming back. Oh, man...

MONTY. Use those glasses, with the cellophane on the top. You can cover them back up tight and put 'em in a drawer. (*Darwin gets a glass, starts to unzip his pants. Stops. Looks at Monty. Pause.*)

DARWIN. You'd like that, wouldn't you?

MONTY. Like what? (*Darwin takes ice bucket, stands in corner, turns his back to Monty.*)

DARWIN. I got my eye on you.

MONTY. What?

DARWIN. I know everything. Just don't think I don't.

MONTY. Did I tell you my brother's growing a beard?

DARWIN. Your brother is cool.

MONTY. The reason I don't have whiskers is because I have different genes, which is what makes me fat and why he isn't. The way your genes are is how your stuck for life. My brother's got a class in that. (*A beat.*) I bet her whole family has those kind of faces.

DARWIN. That's prob'ly how they found each other.

MONTY. Do you think I look like my brother at all? A little bit? (*Pause.*) Do I?

DARWIN. I don't know. (*Darwin sets ice bucket back on bureau.*)

MONTY. Just a little? A very little bit. Darwin?

DARWIN. Why do you ask me stupid questions? How can you look like him if you don't even come from the same family?

MONTY. My mother says they love me as if I did.

DARWIN. That's not being in the family. It's not blood. It's not like blood love. If you don't have the same blood you can't have the same feelings.

MONTY. That's what my brother said. (*He goes to door, listens.*) Guess what? My brother did it to Millicent Whickster.

DARWIN. He dropped Millicent Whickster.

MONTY. No he didn't. He thinks she's hot.

DARWIN. Not where it counts, he said. He dropped her last week.

MONTY. No he didn't.

DARWIN. He told us. He took us out to the lake and bought us beer and drank it and we puked.

MONTY. He did not.

DARWIN. In his Jetta. It was great.

MONTY. He won't let kids ride in his Jetta.

DARWIN. He stuck the cassettes in my lap and said 'You be D.J.'. I played the music all night.

MONTY. That's a lie.

DARWIN. Last Saturday night.

MONTY. He goes out with his friends on Saturday night.

DARWIN. Well. Yeah. That's what he did.

MONTY. But you're not his friend.

DARWIN. He liked my Nike Nuffer's. He said they were like creme jello.

MONTY. But he thinks you're a baby.

DARWIN. Bullshit he does. We traded shoes for the whole night.

MONTY. You're lying! He thinks you're a crybaby asshole tag-along!

DARWIN. Bullshit he does! (*A beat.*) He told me when you thought he was asleep the other night you crawled into bed with him and put your arms around him and held on to him and kissed him on the neck. He said he just pretended to be asleep. He said he could feel you smelling his hair.

MONTY. That's... a...

DARWIN. How would I know about that if that's a lie? (*Pause.*) He said you're queer.

MONTY. I'm... not...

DARWIN. That's what he said, Monty! (*Pause. Monty stands, looks around for his clothes. He moves as if a bit dazed. Slowly starts getting dressed.*) What're you doing? You getting dressed?

MONTY. There's things that mean other things than what they are.

DARWIN. You aren't gonna do it?

MONTY. Leave me alone.

DARWIN. How's that gonna look to everyone?

MONTY. Nobody has to know we were ever here. Nobody has to know anything, Darwin.

DARWIN. Things slip out, Monty. People hear. It's a fact of life. (*Pause.*)

MONTY. Listen to her. Did you ever think someone like that could sing so beautiful? D'you think she knows? D'you think anyone's ever told her?

DARWIN. You want him to think you're a chicken shit,

too? A chicken shit queer?
MONTY. How would he have to know anything?
DARWIN. Because a person can't keep this quiet forever. (*A beat.*)
MONTY. Thanks, Darwin.
DARWIN. Well? If you're gonna —
MONTY. Get out, Darwin. Please. Get out.
DARWIN. I'm trying to help you —
MONTY. Get out. Get out! GET OUT! (*A beat.*)
DARWIN. Hell with you then. Hell with you. (*Darwin starts for door.*)
MONTY. Hey. Darwin.
DARWIN. What?
MONTY. If you love someone you belong to the same family. You can tell my brother that's what *I* said. (*Darwin leaves. Monty sits on the bed in his clothes. Listens to her sing.*) I didn't know she sang so good. (*Monty waits on the bed. Lights fade.*)

* * *

LATE ARRIVAL

by

Theresa Rebeck

Late Arrival was produced at the First Annual Boston Theater Marathon on April 18th, 1999. Sponsored by New Theatre, Inc. Directed by Rick DesRochers.
The cast was as follows:
LILA .... Sharyn Holic
MIMI .... Kim Mansfield

CHARACTERS

LILA
MIMI

PLACE

A room.

LATE ARRIVAL

(*Two women, Lila and Mimi, wait in a room. There is a table and one chair. Mimi fiddles nervously with an unlit cigarette.*)

MIMI. So, are you going to tell her?
LILA. Yes, I'm going to tell her.
MIMI. When?
LILA. I said I'd tell her. I'm going to tell her.
MIMI. Today?
LILA. I don't know.
MIMI. Because you know, she has to be told.
LILA. I know.
MIMI. I mean, she has to be *told*, Lila.
LILA. And I said I'd do it, Mimi.
MIMI. Okay, good.
LILA. Yes. (*Beat.*)
MIMI. Did she say when she was going to get back?
LILA. No. She didn't.
MIMI. (*A burst.*) Because I think it should be today. I do. I haven't said anything before this, because you know, but it's getting, *everyone* knows, except her. And the longer it goes on the worse it's going to be. If she hears it the wrong way? What if someone just tells her? Someone else, I mean. And then she finds out we knew, and we didn't. That could happen. I'm amazed it hasn't happened already.

LILA. Look, you know —
MIMI. What?
LILA. (*Pissed now.*) Why don't you tell her? You're so worked up about this, you tell her. You're the one who saw it.
MIMI. You want me to tell her?
LILA. What I want is — I said I'd tell her, and I will, but you know, this is — fucked, that's what this is. Fucked. You need to back off.
MIMI. Oh, well that was useful. Thank you.
LILA. Oh, Christ.
MIMI. I mean, okay I admit I'm nervous about this. I admit that. But you should have told her. You said you were going to tell her and then you didn't and this has been going on for how long? I mean, I agreed, I did, that you could be the one to do it, not out of fear, god, that is not my concern at all, but because both of us felt it would be easier for her. Better for her.
LILA. (*Cutting her off.*) Yes, it will be better for her because you are turning into a complete whacko on this subject. I mean, what is the big deal? Once she's told, that's it, there's no going back. I mean, it's not exactly going to make her feel better, now is it? So what's the big rush to ruin her life?
MIMI. I am not ruining her life. It's not my fault, I saw what I saw! If I saw it, other people did too, you can bet on that. You saw it too. I'm not the only one.
LILA. I didn't, actually. (*A beat.*)
MIMI. You said you did.
LILA. I thought I did. I'm not so sure now.
MIMI. You said you did. When you told me, *you* told me —
LILA. (*Correcting her.*) I told you what I thought I

saw, and then you told me what you had seen several weeks before that. And it was the similarity of the events that made us wonder if perhaps we shouldn't have a conversation with her. But if I'm not so sure of what I saw, then you had better be very sure. That's all I'm saying.

MIMI. I am sure. It was unmistakable.

LILA. It could not have been a fantasy?

MIMI. What kind of a — why would I fantasize something like that? Something that would hurt her like that, do you think I'm glad that I saw it? I've just been miserable, I've been sick about it ever since and you promised — *You* were the one who said we had to tell her, that was something *I* thought — and now you just — I don't understand why, it's like you're deliberately — (*She stops this time. Lila stares at her.*)

LILA. Deliberately what?

MIMI. I don't know. But this is not right. It's not right. (*Lila considers her. After a moment she reaches into her purse, pulls out a compact, and puts lipstick on. Mimi watches her.*) I think you should go. If you're not going to tell her, you should go, and I, I, I will. But I think it would be better if it was done privately. So you should... she could be back, any minute.

LILA. Then you are going to tell her?

MIMI. (*Upset at this.*) Yes! I don't, just because now, *you're* not so sure, that's not relevant. It doesn't mean anything. I know what I saw. And I think if it were me, if I were her? I would want to know. So I think I just owe it to her, okay.

LILA. (*Cool.*) So, you're going to tell her. And you're going to take responsibility for that.

MIMI. Yes.

LILA. (*Standing to go.*) All right then.

MIMI. It's just that you're not doing it and we've got to do something before she finds out in some horrible way. That is my only concern.

LILA. You've made that clear. (*She heads for the door.*)

MIMI. I will tell her. (*Lila stops, looks over her shoulder.*)

LILA. You just said that.

MIMI. Yes, and I say it again because I mean it. I am going to tell her.

LILA. As soon as she gets here.

MIMI. Yes.

LILA. Regardless of how she's feeling or acting, if she's in a good mood, or a bad mood, maybe someone will be with her, regardless of any of that, you are going to tell her. Today.

MIMI. Well — not if someone's with her. Of course not then.

LILA. Why not?

MIMI. Well, because it's — come on. I could hardly —

LILA. You could hardly what?

MIMI. We agreed —

LILA. I'm not the one questioning the agreement. You're — you have barely shut up since I got here, your anxiety about the fact that she has not yet been told is absolutely filling the room, you're in such a mad rush to tell her that I've been completely *de*monized, unequivocably, asked to *leave*, in fact, because it seems to me that the exercise of caution in this matter is somehow not an *irrelevant* issue. And now you can hardly what, you can hardly be expected to tell her if the circumstances are suddenly found to be not of your liking? You know, this is not about you. Has that occurred to you? The whole reason we — the reason, as you'll recall, that we decided *I* would be the one to tell her, is because it would make it easier on *her*. She is the one who is going to be destroyed by this. Perhaps not destroyed, certainly we hope not destroyed, but there is little question, is there, *is* there, that this is not a happy thing. Not Happy. None of us are Happy. Are we?

MIMI. This isn't helping.

LILA. Well, and god knows, every word out of your mouth has just been a blessing, today. A rain of blessings. Every blessed fucking word. (*They look at each other. Mimi looks away.*) So. Do you still want me to leave? Do you still want to tell her yourself?

MIMI. (*Upset.*) I don't want to tell her! But I want her told!

LILA. Then we're back to where we started, aren't we? (*She takes the unlit cigarette from Mimi, goes to her purse, gets a lighter, and lights it. Mimi watches. After a moment.*)

MIMI. What are you going to say?

LILA. I'm not talking to you about this anymore. (*A beat.*)

MIMI. It's a pretty day.

LILA. Lovely.

MIMI. Maybe that's what's keeping her. The weather.

LILA. (*A warning.*) Mimi.

MIMI. I'm not.

LILA. Good.

MIMI. I thought you quit.

LILA. I did quit. This is not smoking. I am not smoking. (*Lila smokes.*)

MIMI. Okay. (*A beat, then.*) Just cheating, huh. (*Lila looks at her, but doesn't answer.*) You're not smoking, you're cheating. There's a difference. I know that because I used to do that. But I can't cheat. I smoke. Well, you know, you saw it. It was pathetic. Going for days without a cigarette, and then convincing myself that I could have just one. Then just one a day, then two a day, god, counting every drag, this is not what it seems, I'm not really smoking, I'm cheating! So I thought, you know, I did think that just holding onto one, just holding it, was the solution. And now you're sitting there smoking it and whoa, do I — you know. Well, you, maybe you don't, actually, you never seemed to want them as much as I did. Because I really. Anyway. I used to love smoking. I guess that's the way. Those of us who love it, just can't do it. We just can't. (*She seems suddenly defeated by this knowledge. Lila watches her. The lights fade.*)

* * *

BENITA'S CHOICE: HAROLD'S SAY

by

Lois Roach

Benita's Choice: Harold's Say was produced at the First Annual Boston Theater Marathon on April 18th, 1999. Sponsored by Underground Railway Theatre Company. Directed by Lois Roach. The cast was as follows:

BARTENDER .... Naheem Allah
HAROLD .... Dorian Baucum

To Lewis and Helen and Guy

CHARACTERS

THE BARTENDER — (*Black male*) is also the Narrator – the Spirit who see and "thinks" he knows all. He is ageless, but aged with wisdom!

HAROLD — (*Black male – 30's.*) is an UPS worker who has found the love of his life – but is he ready?

TIME
Now.

PLACE
Mr. Brown's Bar-B-Q restaurant.

BENITA'S CHOICE: HAROLD'S SAY

(Harold is at Mr. Brown's Bar-B-Q. He's seated at the bar torturing the Bartender.)

BARTENDER. *(To the audience.)* Oh what tangled webs we weave. Oh what tangled webs we weave. Only to get tangled up in our own shit. *(To Harold.)* You told her how you felt about everything. Dished it out like a man. Said where you stand. *(Harold nods painfully.)*. Man, didn't you say you did the right thing? Got you up here drinking and you don't even know how to drink. Non-drinking man looking sad.

HAROLD. I know I made the right decision. I haven't called her. It was getting too heavy.

BARTENDER. Got to be careful about heavy. Women like heavy man.

HAROLD. Starting to feel a little choked up.

BARTENDER. Like the reins were coming in. First the reins, then the noose.

HAROLD. Like the world as I knew it was gonna be over.

BARTENDER. Soon.

HAROLD. Soon.

BARTENDER. Yeh man. Soon.

HAROLD. You know what I mean.

BARTENDER. I'm right there with you. But the woman always looked so good.

HAROLD. Didn't she though?
BARTENDER. Damn good.
HAROLD. Make you so mad she looked so good. Like she was doing this shit on purpose.
BARTENDER. You know she was. Smell good too.
HAROLD. What chu know about that?
BARTENDER. Anything that looked that good got to smell good too. I assumed.
HAROLD. But I'm doing the right thing.
BARTENDER. It's better this way.
HAROLD. Maybe one day we'll be able to be friends.
BARTENDER. I wouldn't count on that.
HAROLD. No?
BARTENDER. Wouldn't count on that one bit. No sir, no way.
HAROLD. Why not?
BARTENDER. A woman like that probably got lots of friends. You don't want to get lost in the crowd. A woman like that probably got lots of traffic jams outside her house, with friends just stopping by and all. A traffic combustion waiting to happen. No sir. A good looking, good smelling woman like that. No way. No more friends.
HAROLD. I did do the right thing.
BARTENDER. Of course you did. A woman like that would have you wearing the wedding dress. You wouldn't even know your name.
HAROLD. I got things to do. She was getting in my way.
BARTENDER. Absolutely. They do that.
HAROLD. They do that.
BARTENDER. They sure do that. Get all up under your skin and start crawling into your thoughts. You're trying to be the man and get things done. And they just keep getting

BENITA'S CHOICE... 163

in the way. Like a little inchworm coming through your ear. There's no time for your own stuff anymore. And don't try to do nothing. Oh no. They get in your way now. That they do.

HAROLD. They do that. Then they make you see that you got a lot to do. A lot to work on. And you're not sure they'll be around while you're doing it. You just don't feel ready, ya know. You realize how much of a hole you have. And you know they can't fill all of it. No one should.

So now what do you do? You got all this stuff to work on and you still got a hole. And you don't know how long this work is going to take. Women get expectations after a while. I wouldn't be able to meet them. A woman like that makes you look at yourself and then you get all pissed at her. Pissed at her for coming at the wrong time. And I know it's not her fault.

I don't want to be angry at her. I couldn't do that to her.
BARTENDER. So you did what you had to do.
Harold. I sure did.
BARTENDER. You said ciao, see ya, adios, arreva derci, peace out.
HAROLD. Let the door knob hit ya.
Bartender. And?
HAROLD. She said I was scared.
BARTENDER. Scared?
HAROLD. Can you believe that?
BARTENDER. Sounds like some shit my third wife told me. I was scared she said. She may have been right. But the girl's gone now so hey! On to the next. You did the right thing.
HAROLD. I did the right thing. I did.

BARTENDER. You took control of the situation. You did.

HAROLD. I did.

BARTENDER. You did. Would you like a beverage?

HAROLD. Yeh. (*Then stronger.*) Yes! (*Moments of silence as thoughts are gathered.*)

BARTENDER. Whacha' thinking?

HAROLD. How nothing seems to add up. I'm stuck when I'm with her and I'm stuck without her.

BARTENDER. Well, seems like you might not want to be stuck too long my brother. A sister like that gets a chance - she'll move on.

HAROLD. That's part of the problem. Suppose I get in there and she wants to move on?

BARTENDER. Seems like that's always the problem. Best you can do is get in there and try to go the distance. Then if it doesn't work at least you know you tried.

HAROLD. Yeh, but to go the distance and then have it all go bad...

BARTENDER. Hell, if you don't even get in the ring the fight's over and it's all gone bad anyway. You're just getting a little more control over when it goes bad. Right now or maybe down the line. Seems like you bail out now and it's guaranteed gone bad. Make sense?

HAROLD. I think so. But didn't you say before that she would have me wearing the wedding dress? That's all a woman wants to do is own you. Keep you like a pet on a leash. One minute she's kissing you — next minute she's walking you.

BARTENDER. Look — I only give you back what you want to hear. So you can kinda' hear yourself talking to yourself. I don't get paid enough money for that real advice shit.

HAROLD. Thanks a lot. (*Harold gets up, throws down a dollar and goes to leave.*)
BARTENDER. Hey, I try. I will help a brother out though.
HAROLD. How?
BARTENDER. It might be worth working out all this confusion, and brother you got a whole lot of confusion.
HAROLD. And what good will that do?
BARTENDER. Hell if I know. But at least you'd be confused together, and working it out together and struggling through together, so that by the time you're done you're doing a whole helluva lot of making up together or you're just plain through. And you're coming back here to get another bottle of Jack and celebrate 'bout the whole thing being one more sad, tired, sorry ass chapter in your life.
HAROLD. I don't know.
BARTENDER. Sometimes you only get one more chance.
HAROLD. Oh shit.
BARTENDER. Oh shit yeh or shit no? What kinda shit is "oh shit?"
HAROLD. (*He struggles with this.*) Oh shit. Yeh. (*The Bartender slaps him five and sends Harold on his way.*)
BARTENDER. There you go. Be a contender. It's the latest thriller since Manila. It's the bomb getting ready to drop. Peace my brother. Go on out there. And most importantly... Know... (*To the audience.*) I'll be right here on the other side.

* * *

MEN ARE FROM MILWAUKEE, WOMEN ARE FROM PHOENIX

by

M. Lynda Robinson

Men Are From Milwaukee, Women Are From Phoenix was produced at the First Annual Boston Theater Marathon on April 18th, 1999. Sponsored by Lyric West Theatre. Directed by Ronn Smith. The cast was as follows:

HE .... David Ian
SHE .... M. Lynda Robinson

To Lee — When we love the enemy,
we all win the Gender Wars.

CHARACTERS

HE — a male actor
SHE — a female actor

PLACE

Bedroom of He and She

TIME

Evening, the present

MEN ARE FROM MILWAUKEE, WOMEN ARE FROM PHOENIX

(We are in the bedroom of the home of He and She consisting of at least a double bed, night stands, lamp, rug.

At rise: both actors are in bed. He is reading a horror (or science fiction or "action".) book. She has a map of the United States spread out on the bed and a book titled "Men Are from Milwaukee, Women Are from Phoenix." She refers back and forth between the map and the book.)

SHE. (*Reading/summarizing from the book, checking out the locations on the map and tracing them with her finger.*) The premise seems to be that in the long-ago past, all the males on the planet lived in Milwaukee and all the females lived in Phoenix, and they were all very happy. Then a group of the women formed a Riding Club and took their horses North on a trip to find a passageway to Denver and ended up in Milwaukee. There they discovered a strange civilization of tall, hairy people drinking a foamy substance which seemed to make them alternatingly sleepy or loud.

HE. Cars hadn't been invented yet?

SHE. Apparently no one had discovered Detroit yet.

HE. So I assume they met and war was immediately declared. Who had the biggest weapons?

SHE. (*Affectionately.*) No - this a book about love, about how the sexes, being from two different cities, can live together in peace and harmony.

HE. (*Impatiently.*) OK, OK, for the sake of "peace and harmony" let's get going.

SHE. I am going. I'm telling you the origins, the theme, from the Introduction. Look, do you want to read the first chapter?

HE. No, I just want to know how the women got to Milwaukee.

SHE. I just told you - with their Riding Club.

HE. But they didn't have cars yet.

SHE. No — horses, horses! It's an earlier civilization! You aren't listening, you never listen. Please try to listen!

HE. I'm just wondering if they had developed maps or whether they got lost and ended up in Milwaukee.

SHE. What are you saying — that the only way women could possibly have found their way to Milwaukee was by accident?

HE. Well, OK, I'll admit that men don't ask for directions, but they are better drivers. (*Short silence.*)

SHE. Can we get on with this — we haven't even started Chapter One yet.

HE. Sure — you're in charge.

SHE. I'm not "in charge." I'm just reading the First Chapter. (*Puts map on floor.*) You will read the Second Chapter. (*Takes his book away from him and puts it on bedside table.*) If you sit like that, you're going to hurt your back again.

HE. Like I said, you're in charge. (*He shifts position. Short silence.*)

SHE. (*Reading from the book.*) Chapter One: Mr. "I Know It All" and Ms. "You Don't Know Anything" (*Short silence. They look at each other. She continues reading.*) The greatest complaint that women have about men is that they don't listen. (*She gives him a look.*) The greatest complaint that men have about women is that they take control. (*He is biting his nails. Without even looking, she takes his hand away from his mouth & moves it down to his side. He gives her a look. She doesn't notice it. Continues reading.*) In Phoenix, when women are scared or upset or lonely, they talk to other Phoenixians about it and the other Phoenixians all listen. They enjoy this and get comfort and knowledge from it.

HE. By complaining and telling everyone their problems?

SHE. (*Sighs, continues reading.*) In Milwaukee, when men are scared or upset or lonely, they go to their caves until they feel strong, and know that it's safe to come out because no other Milwaukean saw them depressed and living in the same clothes for consecutive days. They enjoy this and get comfort from the strategy games they play while in hibernation.

HE. Is there supposed to be something wrong with that?

SHE. I don't think this is about right or wrong — it's about understanding the way in which genders are different so that we can learn to communicate.

HE. Well, the people in Phoenix need to learn to be alone, and if they can't figure it out for themselves, then they need to just find a professional who can fix whatever it is that's wrong.

SHE. (*Reading.*) In Milwaukee, all the male humans like to solve things. But Milwaukeans keep problems to themselves. It is a sign of weakness to ask for help.

However, if a Milwaukean can't figure something out, it is a sign of strength to consult an expert in the field. This is why when female humans from Phoenix talk about their problems, Milwaukeans put on their "I'll Fix-It" hat and offer expert advice. (*Short silence.*)

HE. Was this book written by a man or a woman?

SHE. I don't know. (*She looks at the book cover for the author's name.*) Someone named Skye Labyrinthe. (*He looks at her questioningly.*) It's Skye with an "e." (*He looks at her questioningly again.*)

SHE. It's also Labyrinthe with an "e." (*Pause.*) It could be a man or a woman.

HE. It could be someone who's still wearing beads and living in a commune.

SHE. Or it could be someone who's an observer of human nature and has learned through experience — maybe it's a counselor — maybe it's someone who lives in Florida in a condo! Who cares! It seems to be someone with helpful information. Do you want me to find the bio?!

HE. I'll find it — give me the book.

SHE. No — this is a diversion because you really don't want to do this! You're looking for a reason to discredit, rather than being open to change!

HE. You're right — I don't want to change! I just want to see the bio! Give me the book!

SHE. No! (*They struggle over the book. Note to Director: choreograph a short, comical, physical struggle here — on the bed, around the room, whatever — but ending up back on the bed. He wins — holds the book out where she can't reach it and reads loudly and triumphantly.*)

HE. Skye Labyrinthe spent twenty years in Turkey as Operations Manager of the Exxon Global Shipping and

Motivation Departments. Skye now lives in Buffalo and runs the School of Human Encounter and Aromatherapy. (*Silence.*)

SHE. Is there a photo? (*They both look.*)

HE. No. (*They both look puzzled. He hands her the book.*)

SHE. (*Begins to read.*) In Phoenix ...

HE. (*Interrupting.*) I think it's a woman.

SHE. Why? Because men don't care if they smell good?

HE. No. Because a real man would have changed his name to something like Storm Labyrinthe or Lightning Rod Labyrinthe.

SHE. (*Closes book.*) I'm not going to read any more if you're going to make fun of this — this isn't funny. (*She starts to get upset.*) Do you think this is easy? To agree to bare one's soul? To appear vulnerable before someone you love? To try to reach out and then be cruelly taunted? (*Searching for the words to accurately/honestly express her feelings.*) It's like a ... a ... butterfly ... pushing and pushing it's way out of a cocoon — finally seeing the sunlight and ... and ... flowers ... and spreading it's wings to greet life — and getting smashed with a tennis racquet!

HE. I don't play tennis.

SHE. (*Screams loudly. Then tries to calm herself.*) Can't you just listen to me?

HE. I heard exactly what you said — moths rise to the flame and get hit by tennis racquets. (*A pause.*)

SHE. (*Defeated.*) This isn't going to work. (*She throws the book down and starts to leave, crawling off his side of the bed.*)

HE. Why are you so upset? Don't be upset!

SHE. (*Stops, faces him.*) Don't tell me not to be upset! I'm upset, OK? (*Pacing around back to her side of the bed. Angry/hurt.*) This is upsetting, so I'm upset!

HE. Why — because of a book?

SHE. No, not because of a book — because of your reaction! It's upsetting so I'm upset! (*Bursts into tears, gets back into bed on her side, pulling covers over her.*) Just let me be upset! (*Sobs under the covers.*)

HE. (*Imploring.*) Listen, we don't need this book. This person doesn't know anything about us. This person thinks that he or she can categorize male behavior and female behavior. This person is just trying to make money from people who are weak and can't think for themselves! What ever happened to the individual — the right to be free!! (*He picks up the book.*) Look, I'll open to any page and I guarantee you whatever it says is generalized and won't have anything to do with us. (*She sticks her head out from under the covers. He opens to a random page and reads.*) Why do men and women argue? Women often fight for their right to be upset and men often fight for their right to express their freedom. (*Silence. They both look at each other. They both sit up on the bed next to each other. He picks up the book and begins reading.*)

HE. Chapter Two: "How to Avoid an Argument." (*They look at each other. The lights go out.*)

* * *

DUET FOR SHY PEOPLE
A ten-minute musical

Book and Lyrics by Richard Schotter
Music by Michael Kosarin

176 THE BOSTON THEATER MARATHON

Duet for Shy People was first performed at the BMI-Lehman Engel Musical Theatre Workshop on May 17, 1993. The cast was as follows:
JANE .... Susan Egan
JOE .... Adam Grupper

Duet for Shy People was produced at the First Annual Boston Theater Marathon on April 18th, 1999. Sponsored by North Shore Music Theatre. Directed by Craig Foley. The cast was as follows:
JANE .... Merle Perkins
JOE .... Chip Phillips
MUSICAL DIRECTOR .... Douglas Horner

CHARACTERS

JOE — a Young man.
JANE — a Young woman.
MUSICAL DIRECTOR

TIME
Now.

PLACE
Manhattan.

DUET FOR SHY PEOPLE

I. THEY MEET

JOE.
HI.

JANE.
HI.

JOE.
I'M SHY.

JANE.
SO AM I.

JOE.
GOOD-BYE.

JANE.
GOOD-BYE.

BOTH.
GOOD-BYE.

JOE.
HOW DO YOU DO?

JANE.
FINE, AND YOU?

JOE.
I DO FINE TOO.

JANE.
I'M GLAD YOU DO.

JOE.
JUST CAME FROM LUNCH.

JANE.
OH, I DID TOO.
TUNA PLATTER.

JOE.
IRISH STEW.

JANE.
I LOVE A STEW.

JOE.
STEW'S SOOTHING WHEN YOU'RE BLUE.
NICE MEETING YOU.

JANE.
I BETTER GO.

JOE.
MY NAME IS JOE.
CAN YOU WAIT?

JANE.
I'M RUNNING LATE.

JOE.
WELL, SO AM I.

JANE.
WELL THEN, GOOD-BYE.

JOE.
WHAT IS YOUR NAME?

JANE.
MY NAME IS JANE.

JOE.
LOVELY NAME.

JANE.
I THINK IT'S PLAIN.

JOE.
I WORK NEARBY.

JANE.
OH, SO DO I.

JOE.
NBC?

JANE.
NO, NOT TV.

JOE.
GIVE ME A HINT.

JANE.
I WORK IN PRINT.

JOE.
YOU'VE GOT THE LOOKS.

JANE.
NO, SELLING BOOKS.

JOE.
MUST RUN ALONG.

JANE.
IS SOMETHING WRONG?

JOE.
NOT AT ALL,
I LOVE BOOKS.

JANE.
SO DO I.
BECAUSE I'M SHY.
I HAVE TO GO.
IT'S GETTING LATE.
SEE YOU JOE.

JOE.
MY BOSS WON'T WAIT.
IT'S BEEN...

JANE.
NICE.

JOE.
WOULD YOU?

JANE.
WHAT?

JOE.
LIKE TO...

JANE.
YES?

JOE.
I'M SHY.

JANE.
SO AM I.

BOTH.
GOOD-BYE.

II. JOE PONDERS

JOE.
THERE I GO AGAIN,
THE UNROMANTIC HERO.
ALL PREPARED AND THEN
OVERCOME BY FEAR.

182 THE BOSTON THEATER MARATHON

SCALE OF ONE TO TEN,
I'M SOMEWHERE UNDER ZERO,
CAN SOMEONE TELL ME WHEN
MY COURAGE MIGHT APPEAR?

WHAT I'VE GOT TO DO
IS START A CONVERSATION.
MAKE A JOKE OF TWO,
PASS THE TIME OF DAY.
THEN, BEFORE I'M THROUGH,
EXTEND AN INVITATION,
"MIND IF I CALL YOU,"
IS HARD FOR ME TO SAY.

IF I WERE FREE AND EASY
FOR JUST A HALF AN HOUR,
I'D BLITHELY CALL HER NAME
AND LOOK HER STRAIGHT IN THE EYE.
I'D PLAY IT LIGHT AND BREEZY,
IN SOME ROMANTIC BOWER,
AND SET HER HEART AFLAME.
I'VE GOT TO TRY!

MY FATE HAS BEEN DECREED,
THIS TIME I REALLY KNOW IT,
SHE EVEN LOVES TO READ.
I BET SHE'S VERY BRIGHT.
SHE'S EVERYTHING I NEED;
I CAN'T AFFORD TO BLOW IT.
I'LL SHOW HER HOW I FEEL.
I'LL TRY WITH ALL MY MIGHT
TO REACH OUT AND REVEAL
WHAT'S HIDDEN OUT OF SIGHT.

DUET FOR SHY PEOPLE 183

NO PAINFUL MASQUERADE,
FINALLY NOT AFRAID TO TRY,
AND FLY.
NO TIME TO HESITATE,
WAIT OR WONDER WHY.
THE HOUR'S GETTING LATE,
I'VE GOT TO TRY
NEXT TIME SHE PASSES BY.

III. SHE PONDERS

JANE.
I SAY HELLO,
I WONDER WHAT HE'LL THINK.
HE STARTS TO SMILE,
MY HEART BEGINS TO SINK.
HE OFFERS WINE,
IS THAT WHAT I SHOULD DRINK?
I NEVER KNOW,
AND SO,
I DO NOTHING.

HE LOOKS MY WAY,
I WONDER HOW I LOOK.
HE LOOKS AGAIN,
I STARE INTO MY BOOK.
HE PASSES BY,
I WRIGGLE ON A HOOK.
I TRY TO SPEAK,
FEEL WEAK,
AND SAY NOTHING.

NOTHING
IS WHAT COMES FROM NOTHING.
NO ADVENTURES,
YEARS PASS BY.
SOMETHING
NEEDS TO COME FROM ONE THING,
A SIMPLE SMILE OR TWO, A WORD,
A SIGH.

SOMETIMES I SIGH,
WHEN I THINK OF ROMANCE.
AND ALL THE TIMES,
I STAYED HOME FROM THE DANCE.
IF I DON'T TRY,
IF I DON'T TAKE A CHANCE,
I'LL SIMPLY WAIT
TOO LATE, AND HAVE NOTHING.

NOTHING
EVER COMES FROM NOTHING.
NO ADVENTURES,
YEARS ROLL ON.
SOMETHING
HAS TO COME FROM SOMETHING.
A MOMENT LIVED
BEFORE THE MOMENT'S GONE.
I LIKE HIS EYES,
THEY SPARKLE WHEN HE SPEAKS.
HE HARDLY SPEAKS,
BUT THAT'S NO BIG SURPRISE.
BUT WHEN HE DOES
I'M SURE HE ISN'T WEAK.
I KNOW HE'S VERY STRONG.

DUET FOR SHY PEOPLE

HE DOESN'T HAVE TO SPEAK.
HE LETS ME KNOW
IN OTHER WAYS HE SHOWS ME.
THE MORE HE SHOWS,
THE MORE LOVE GROWS.
IF NOTHING'S SAID,
ROMANCE IS DEAD.
THE TIME IS HERE.
YOU'RE IN THE CLEAR.
NOTHING TO FEAR.

IV. THEY MEET AGAIN

JOE. (*Spoken.*) This is it, Joe. You're going to stand in front of this store until you see her. And when you do, zero hour has arrived. (*Singing.*)
THERE SHE IS,
DOWN THE STREET.
THIS IS IT,
NOW OR NEVER.

JANE.
THERE HE IS,
LOOKING SWEET.
BE SINCERE,
DON'T GET CLEVER.

JOE.
BE YOURSELF.
DON'T BE COOL.
YOU'D BETTER STOP PLAYING MACHO.

JANE.
HOW'S MY DRESS?
WHAT A FOOL.
WHY'D I EAT
THAT GAZPACHO
AT LUNCH?

JOE.
JUST RELAX,
SETTLE DOWN.
DON'T FORGET
NOT TO PANIC.

JANE.
GET A GRIP.
BITE YOUR LIP.
NO NEED TO BE
QUITE SO MANIC.

JOE.
HERE SHE COMES.
NOW'S THE TIME.
STEP RIGHT UP
AND DELIVER.

JANE.
NOW MY SLIP
STARTS TO CLIMB.
MY KNEES ARE STARTING
TO SHIVER
BELOW.

DUET FOR SHY PEOPLE

JOE.
IS THERE GARLIC ON MY BREATH?
THIS IS WORSE THAN FACING DEATH.

BOTH.
BUT HERE WE GO.

JOE.
HELLO.

JANE.
HELLO. (*The following overlaps somewhat.*)

JOE.	JANE.
MY NAME'S JOE.	YES, I KNOW.
JOE.	JANE.
YOUR NAME'S JANE.	CAN'T COMPLAIN.
JOE.	JANE.
I MEANT TO SAY.	OH, THAT'S OK.
JOE.	JANE.
LOVELY DAY	VERY NICE.
JOE.	JANE.
FIRST OF MAY	PARADISE.
JOE.	JANE.
I LIKE IT HERE.	THE AIR IS CLEAR.

JOE.
JANE?

JANE.
YES?
JOE?

JOE.
YES?

JANE.
I BETTER GO.

JOE.
DON'T GO AWAY.

JANE.
WHAT'S THAT YOU SAY?

JOE.
I WISH YOU'D SAY.

JANE.
IF IT'S OK.

JOE.
BELIEVE ME, IT'S OK.

JANE.
OK, I'LL STAY.

JOE.
JANE?

JANE.
YES?

JOE.
I WONDER...

JANE.
YES...

JOE.
I'M THINKING...

JANE.
TRUE...

JOE.
I MEAN...

JANE.
YOU GUESS...

JOE.
THAT ME AND YOU...
MIGHT LIKE TO...

JANE.
YES?

JOE.
MIGHT LIKE TO GO...

JANE.
YES. YES...

JOE.
I'M TRYING. OH, GOD, I AM TRYING.

JANE.
I'M DYING. OH, GOD, I AM DYING
TO KNOW

JOE.
MIGHT LLL...

JANE.
JUST SAY IT, JOE!

JOE.
TO A POETRY READING TONIGHT AT THE Y.

JANE.
THE CONFESSIONAL POETS FROM LOWELL TO BLY.

JOE.
DON'T TELL ME THAT YOU LIKE POETRY?

JANE.
A POET IS WHAT I WANT TO BE.

JOE.
IF IT'S NOT A GOOD NIGHT TO...

JANE.
I WAS ABOUT TO INVITE YOU...

DUET FOR SHY PEOPLE

JOE.
IT'S JUST A SUGGESTION...

JANE.
WITHOUT ANY QUESTION...

JOE.
IF IT ISN'T TOO MUCH OF A TASK... ?

JANE.
I WAS WONDERING WHEN YOU WOULD ASK ME.

JOE.
THEN YOU'LL COME?

JANE.
BE DELIGHTED.

JOE.
I FEEL DUMB.

JANE.
I'M EXCITED.

JOE.
TEN OF EIGHT.

JANE.
AT THE DOOR?

JOE.
IT'S A DATE!

JANE.
SOMETHING MORE?

JOE.
THIS IS LIVING, FEEL LIKE GIVING YOU A KISS!

JANE.
YOU MEAN SOMETHING LIKE THIS? (*They awkwardly kiss.*)

V. FINALE

BOTH.
WE'VE BEEN TOGETHER
FOR EIGHT WEEKS NOW.

JANE.
EIGHT WEEKS WITH BARELY A BREAK.

JOE.
I'M NEARLY FINISHED WITH IRVING HOWE.

JANE.
HALFWAY THROUGH FINNEGAN'S WAKE.

BOTH.
IN BETWEEN READING
THERE'S JUST ENOUGH TIME
FOR A KISS OR TWO OR THREE.

DUET FOR SHY PEOPLE

JOE.
SHE HAS A TALENT FOR TURNING A RHYME.

JANE.
HE INSPIRES POETRY.

BOTH.
AND THAT IS THE STORY
OF JANE AND JOE.

JOE.
JANE DIDN'T REFRAIN.

JANE.
JOE SAID HELLO.

BOTH.
WHATEVER HAPPENED
TO JOE AND JANE?
IF YOU'D LIKE TO KNOW,
THEN WE'LL EXPLAIN.
JOSEPH AND JANE GOT MARRIED
ONE FINE DAY.
THE TENTH OF MAY.
AFTER TEN YEARS
HERE'S JANE AND JOE.

JOE.
A COTTAGE IN MAINE.

JANE.
THE POEMS FLOW.

BOTH.
FOUR LITTLE KIDS
HAVE JOE AND JANE,

JANE.
WHITMAN AND DYLAN,

JOE.
BLAKE,

JANE.
AND TWAIN.

BOTH.
THEIR LIFE HAS BEEN A BOOKWORM'S HOLIDAY.

JOE.
WHAT CAN YOU SAY ABOUT JANE AND JOE?
IT'S ONE OF THOSE STORIES THAT GO TO SHOW
THAT SHY

JANE.
PLUS SHY

JOE.
CAN SOMETIMES FIND A WAY.

JANE.
WHAT MORE TO SAY?
NOW'S THE TIME TO SAY...

JOE.
WHAT?

JANE.
GOOD-BYE.

JOE.
WE CAN'T.

JANE.
I KNOW.

BOTH.
WHY?
BECAUSE WE'RE SHY.

* * *

QUE SERA, SERA

by

Katherine Snodgrass

198 THE BOSTON THEATER MARATHON

Que Sera, Sera was produced at the First Annual Boston Theater Marathon on April 18th, 1999. Sponsored by Boston Playwrights Theatre. Directed by Kate Snodgrass. The cast was as follows:
ANNE .... Dossy Peabody
MICHAEL .... Robert Pemberton

Que Sera, Sera is also published in A Grand Entrance: Scenes And Monologues For Mature Actors, Dramatic Publishing Company, Woodstock, Illinois.

CHARACTERS

ANNE — a slightly older leading lady.
MICHAEL — a slightly younger leading man.

TIME
Early New Year's Day, 1997.

PLACE
The living room of Anne's New York apartment.

QUE SERA, SERA

(*Anne sits, staring into space. A door closes offstage, and she rouses herself — happy, happy, happy. She pours out one glass as Michael enters.*)

ANNE. Happy 1997! (*Singing...*) SHOULD AULD ACQUAINTANCE BE FORGOT... (*Spoken.*) Wasn't that fun?
MICHAEL. Hmmm.
ANNE. A wonderful party. I hadn't seen the Henderson's in years! (*Laughing...*) Oh, but I thought Mal was going to keel over, didn't you? It was all those clams or paté or... What was that green gunk on toast? Some organ.
MICHAEL. I don't know.
ANNE. And Martha Pittinger kept singing! Oh, my gaa-awd, Arty told her she sounded like what's-her-name, you know, who sang that doggie song!
MICHAEL. No.
ANNE. Peggy Lee? The doggie in the window. Who sang that?
MICHAEL. I don't know.
ANNE. And Martha kept barking! Arf-arf. (*Singing...*) HOW MUCH — Was it Patti Page?
MICHAEL. Before my time, I think.
ANNE. Oh, everybody should know that one! The dog's

for sale, and he's in the window, and then he wags his tail and goes arf-arf. Julie London? It can't be.

MICHAEL. It's from the fifties.

ANNE. Doris Day.

MICHAEL. That famous decade of which I have no personal recollection and, therefore, no valid opinion of its worth. (*That stops her.*) That's what you've been trying to tell me all night, isn't it? I wasn't alive in the Renaissance, which we all know was the 1950s, so I'm unpresentable to your battery of friends — and if I had just known who Munkotani was —

ANNE. Mantovani.

MICHAEL. — then I could pass as your 'date', I could be a 'contender'. However, I wasn't born until 1960, that's Six-Oh, which means I don't give a damn about Doris Day, I never thought Sid Caesar was funny, and I don't remember where I was when Kennedy was shot because I was three, count 'em, THREE YEARS OLD! (*Silence.*)

ANNE. I wish you hadn't told me that.

MICHAEL. Don't tell me you didn't know.

ANNE. I thought everyone loved Sid Caesar.

MICHAEL. No. Not this superficial, brain-dead product of the video cartel. But then, I don't know what's funny, do I? — without Show of Shows and Carl Reiner to hit me on the head with it!

ANNE. Oh, we've been playing catch-up on the kinoscopes.

MICHAEL. No, *we* — that is, you and I — have been humping like bunnies for the past three weeks, so when I want to catch up on the 'olden' times, I go ask my Mom. (*Pause.*) I'm sorry. I didn't mean... I'm sorry.

ANNE. No, I suppose I could be your mother. I've played Juliet. What was she — thirteen? Fourteen?

MICHAEL. You couldn't be my —
ANNE. I played Jocasta at the Public, but I hated that Oedipus.
MICHAEL. You couldn't be my mother —
ANNE. No, actually, I could be if I had just met —
MICHAEL. No, no, Anne, you —
ANNE. — Bob Bettis when I was eleven instead of fifteen —
MICHAEL. Anne, will you listen to —
ANNE. — and he'd stolen his father's hooch from the liquor cabinet —
MICHAEL. WILL YOU LISTEN TO ME? (*Silence.*) Who am I to you?
ANNE. Who do you want to be?
MICHAEL. We've been going out, right?
ANNE. Right.
MICHAEL. We... get along, right?
ANNE. Right.
MICHAEL. I want to know what I can expect in the future. (*He waits.*) Do you think we have a future, or... ?
ANNE. Or am I just interested in your body? (*Beat.*) Well... What's your name again? (*He starts to go.*) Mikey, I'm kidding!
MICHAEL. No. (*Turning back.*) Not 'Mikey'. I prefer the adult version at this juncture. 'Mike' or 'Michael', but no 'Mikey'.
ANNE. Mike. Michael, I'm sorry, I didn't mean — ! I'm sorry. You and I, we have absolutely... almost nothing in common. I mean, you live in a nine-to-five world, you grew up with the Brady Bunch. I was weaned on Imogene Coca. And don't say 'Who's that?' You haven't even seen me on stage. I'm heading out of Leading Lady into... Age doesn't mean you lose your fear, you know. If anything,

you get more afraid because you're closer to... losing your teeth.

MICHAEL. Your teeth look fine.

ANNE. They should, they're not mine. Oh my God, I'm living a cliché! You'd think after thirty years in this business, I'd be living a better play! 'Older woman seduces younger man who leaves her heartbroken, weeping, on the edge of despair.' Merde, it's a Melodrama!

MICHAEL. Tennessee Williams.

ANNE. Oh, please, that is such a male fantasy! Blanche did not seduce Stanley.

MICHAEL. I meant Sweet Bird of Youth.

ANNE. Sweet Bird of — ! (*Beat.*) As I recall, that ended in castration. And since when do you know so much about it, anyway? You seem to have picked up quite a few theatre tidbits in Joseph's office. You'd think my own agent would protect me from — ! Now he's getting you to read plays? I thought you were his accountant.

MICHAEL. Maybe he falls in love with her.

ANNE. Joseph?

MICHAEL. The younger man. With the older woman. He's not that much younger, remember, she just thinks he is.

ANNE. Believe me, she knows to the day.

MICHAEL. I'm not that much younger than you. I'm forty-two.

ANNE. Your driver's license says —

MICHAEL. I lied. (*Beat.*) You checked my driver's license?

ANNE. You lied?

MICHAEL. I'm forty-two. That would make me nine when Kennedy died. I was in Mrs. Hoag's fifth grade art class coloring 'John Glenn In Space' when the news came

QUE SERA, SERA

down the pike.

ANNE. You lied? (*Shocked.*) To the Motor Vehicle Department? Why?

MICHAEL. You're not the only one who's embarrassed.

ANNE. I'm not embarrassed about — !

MICHAEL. Our future, Anne. I want to know about our future.

ANNE. Our future. (*Pause.*)

MICHAEL. It's not that difficult a question.

ANNE. No, I'm just having a Chekovian moment.

MICHAEL. Which reminds me... I have to tell you about working at the agency.

ANNE. I knew it. You're not an accountant.

MICHAEL. Yes. No. I mean, I am an accountant, and I have been for ten years. But I'm not just a C.P.A.

ANNE. You're working in an agent's office, you're embarrassed about your age, you're reading Tennessee Will — ! Oh my God, my God! YOU'RE AN ACTOR!

MICHAEL. No, no, don't worry, it's nothing like that. Really.

ANNE. N-n-no? You're not — ?

MICHAEL. No. Really.

ANNE. You're not an — ?

MICHAEL. NO.

ANNE. Oh, thank you! Thank God.

MICHAEL. I'm a playwright. (*Silence.*)

ANNE. You're a playwright. (*Beat.*) For the theatre? (*New idea, solicitious...*) Is this your way of telling me you belong to AA?

MICHAEL. No. No, no.

ANNE. No, I see. A playwright. You're the one who drops cigarette ashes in my dressing room? And gives me line-readings after opening night?

MICHAEL. Well, I'm trying to be.

ANNE. And you can stop this second, because — ! Oh, no, wait! Writers — Their lives are fodder for — ? Oh my God, you're writing as we speak! Aren't you, aren't you, don't deny it!

MICHAEL. I don't know. (*Beat.*) Of course not!

ANNE. Did you think I could help you, is that it? That if you went out with me, that somehow I could — I could —

MICHAEL. No! No. You couldn't get my plays produced anyway.

ANNE. Oh, really. And why is that?

MICHAEL. Because they're Absurd. (*Beat.*) With a capital "A"? Like Beckett, Pinter, Ionesco —

ANNE. I'm familiar with Absurd.

MICHAEL. And I did see you on stage.

ANNE. You saw... ?

MICHAEL. In Six Characters. You wore a black dress slit up to here and you had long red hair that ran down your back like... like... like...

ANNE. A wig?

MICHAEL. — a torch! And when you spoke, fire came out of your mouth. You were brave and unforgiving and the most beautiful thing I'd ever seen. When you left the stage, the light left with you. I couldn't take my eyes off you. I still can't. Don't you know you're breaking my heart? (*Pause.*)

ANNE. Older woman seduces younger man who leaves her heartbroken...

MICHAEL. Are you heartbroken?

ANNE. Are you 42?

MICHAEL. Yes. And no. In the theatre, reality is mutable and subject to change... (*He gives up.*) I'm thirty-six. I was three when Kennedy was shot. I'm a playwright. I have a day job — and I thank God for it because it's how I met you — but I write for the stage. I believe in the power of words, and I love actors as the heart and the soul of the theatre. I'm in love with one actor in particular.

ANNE. She's afraid, you see. She's afraid that one day she'll wake up, and she'll see you watching her in the mirror, and she won't be brave or firey or even pretty. But I will be me. And that won't be enough for you. I'm afraid in the end I'll be alone.

MICHAEL. I can't tell the future, Anne. I don't know what will be. But I know everything about what is. If you think you know so much... Where will you be... (*Deep breath because this is important.*) ...if I can't write a good play? (*Silence.*)

ANNE. I am going to be so in love with you. (*They kiss as... Lights fade.*)

* * *

CHANCE OF YOUR LIFE

by

Brandon Toropov

Chance of Your Life premiered at the First Annual Boston Theater Marathon on April 18th, 1999. Sponsored by Portland Stage Company. Directed by Betsy Carpenter. The cast was as follows:
STEWARDESS .... Kippy Goldfarb
JACK .... Brandon Toropov

CHARACTERS

JACK
STEWARDESS

SETTING

A seat in business class.

CHANCE OF YOUR LIFE

(Minimal scenery suggests the interior of a passenger airplane. The Stewardess off right, back to the audience. Jack stage left talking into a small personal tape recorder. Although he is "in" the airplane set, he is in fact making notes while waiting to board.)

JACK. *(To recorder.)* Leaves bobbing on dark water by the bridge, wearing themselves away. Stepping into the shower with her on Cape Cod the morning after we first slept together. Shaking her small and smooth and wet and attacking body loose from me while we swam at the YMCA. Her hand sweeping everything into place as she cleared off a table in our apartment before a party. A street we crossed during a trip to New York City seven years ago, en route to a bakery she favored. The greatest croissants in — *(Silence.)* Persistent recall of apparently random events with only occasional appearance of deeper cohesive sequences.

STEWARDESS. Ladies and gentlemen, this is United Arlines flight 1764.

JACK. The sound of my mind slipping ever further from its puny moorings. *(Pause.)* JUST WANT A GLIMPSE OF A CONNECTION.

STEWARDESS. *(She turns to face him.)* We will be flying direct to Boston's Logan Airport. Please turn off all pagers, cell phones, and electronic devices at this time. (*Pause. He clicks off the recorder. Without really meaning to, he has "entered the airplane." She continues in a different tone.*) Darling.

JACK. (*Motionless for a moment. Stares at her, begins to move forward.*) Excuse me. (*Brushes past imaginary passengers, checks row, takes his seat. His eyes fixed on her.*)

STEWARDESS. We certainly do appreciate your choice to fly with United today. The Boeing 747 aircraft in which we'll be traveling does have some important safety features; please listen carefully to the flight attendant nearest you, she'll help you become familiar with the most important important important important important that we go to the Ryans' party tonight, Jack. Whether we feel like it or not. (*Silence. He stands up.*) In the event of an emergency, follow instructions. Follow instructions. Follow instructions. Just have to pay attention. Right? Anyway it's a journey over water. Because the bridge, right? Remember the bridge on the way to the Ryans'? Right. So it's a special journey. (*Pause.*)

JACK. They all —

STEWARDESS. They all are, Jack, all of them special journeys, we are all embarked on momentous important journeys, the journeys of a moment or two to to to to to familiarize yourself with the seat belt. (*Little pause. Tactfully.*) Please take a seat, sir. (*Silence. He takes his seat.*) To connect the two halves, place the buckle in the slot until you hear it click. Your seat belt should be fastened snugly across your lap to connect connect connect with him after work a couple of evenings, he's a very nice guy, quite sharp, Steve has a lot of faith in him. So listen ... are we... ? Do you have any...

CHANCE OF YOUR LIFE 211

JACK. (*Catching on.*) No, let's go, fine, to the party, to the... Faye... I've missed you... I mean, I missed you today...

STEWARDESS. In the unlikely event of a loss of cabin pressure, an oxygen mask will drop from the compartment above you. Breathe normally and slowly, a step at a time, because because because because because because...

JACK. Because...

STEWARDESS. Because there are likely to be some changes at work. Actually I think Bill Ryan may end up being my supervisor on some things. (*Silence.*) Honey, are you okay? Ironed your slacks. We're going to be late. Chance of your life, every trip is. Sometimes we know it, sometimes we don't know as much as... as... as... (*Continues repeating it quietly.*)

JACK. Right. Sometimes we... But he just signed on, didn't he? I thought you...

STEWARDESS. (*Interrupting.*)... as... as your seat cushion also serves as a flotation device. Please locate the exit closest to you, and note that the closest exit may be behind you. Please please please please honey I'll drive to the party. Jack you know you don't like to drive. I'll drive. Listen I think we should celebrate. Because listen I've got some good news. (*Pause as he looks at her expectantly.*) If your tray is in its upright and locked position, you may have once been a prime candidate for a chronic karmic-dependent cycle with an unclassified life form. Flashbacks involving important human relationships typically mark a key point of transition; expect emotional turbulence from unusual sources. If your tray is not in its upright and locked position, you may have once been a prime candidate for a chronic karmic-dependent cycle with an unclassified life form. Flashbacks involving important human relationships typically mark a key point of transition; expect emotional turbulence from unusual sources. (*Silence.*)

JACK. You were saying something about good news.

STEWARDESS. Repetitive messages also mark repetitive messages also mark repetitive messages also mark repetitive messages also mark repetitive messages also mark ...

JACK. Honey. What kind of good news?

STEWARDESS. Listen Jack I'm going to have a baby. I know. Can you believe it I know. (*Silence.*) Chance of our lives, right?

JACK. Oh my God are you serious? Oh Jesus that's wonderful, Faye. Faye this is a whole new...

STEWARDESS. Look. Look at me. Do I look any different? Look look look look look look around you. If you are seated in an exit row seat, you may be called upon to assist in an emergency. Follow the directions directions directions directions directions that the doctor, you know seemed very concerned about me following, very, foreheadwrinkled you know. I'm high risk all of a sudden. High risk. HAH! If he KNEW, right? If he KNEW! I mean, please...

JACK. How long have you known? I mean who else have you... ah, never mind, this is GREAT, Faye...

STEWARDESS. ... please read the card in the seat pocket pocket pocket pocket, your car keys, aren't they in your coat pocket? Misplaced mine. Okay let's go. We're going to be late. Chance of your your —

JACK. (*Overlapping on "late".*) Okay, let's go. Chance of your life. Every trip you make, whether you know it or —

STEWARDESS. ... your carry-on luggage. Federal regulations prohibit smoking smoking smoking, so I'm lucky I quit last year, right? And of course mother's in for the shock of the year, she thought I'd never do it. You know, she saw me hit thirty-seven and figured there was no chance. I'm high risk. I'm high risk now. HAH! If he KNEW, right? I'm not either driving too fast. Was that the exit... exits...

JACK. Okay, fine. Okay, fine. Okay, fine, Faye, fine —

STEWARDESS. ... exits are heavy and may be difficult to manipulate. Please keep keep keep an eye on me. Day by day. Anyway this stuff with work, listen Jack, I think I want to quit my job, at least take a leave of absence, do more freelance stuff. I'm not either going too fast. You must... you must...

JACK. Okay, fine, but watch the, I know you're excited but watch the...

STEWARDESS. ... you must be willing and able to perform all the functions shown and described on the cards, catalogs, display units, more freelance stuff, I already talked to Steve about it, just sort of hintingly you know, not saying why, but I think it could work HONEY I AM NOT GOING TOO FAST IT'S PREVAILING SPEED OF THE SURROUNDING TRAFFIC. You're so funny. I mean, for someone who, for someone, for...

JACK. Okay, fine. So freelancing, Jesus, can you do that? I mean I know we can do that but can you do that? Do you want to do that? Is that what you want to do?

STEWARDESS. ... for reseating if you cannot meet the selection criteria; if you have a nondiscernable condition that will prevent you from performing the applicable function; you may suffer bodily harm as the result of performing one or more of the functions; you do not wish to perform the functions; or if you are currently undergoing a frank psychotic episode. (*Silence.*)

JACK. What? (*Silence.*) This is it, this is it... I've really ...

STEWARDESS. Yeah, Jack, this is it. It's for real now, isn't it? Please say you're happy. Look me in the eye and say it. Please please please oh please say you're happy I want you to be happy please please please...

JACK. Yeah. Oh, yeah. Chance of your —

STEWARDESS. Please observe the fasten seat belt sign when it is illuminated. Federal law prohibits tampering with, disabling, or destroying any smoke detector in in in in time for Christmas. Right, chance of your life, hah, like I always say. (*Laughs.*) This is the chance of our lives, Jack, this is the trip! Hah. Christ, we're late. (*Silence.*)

JACK. Hey can anyone on the airplane hear any of this? (*Silence. She does not respond.*) You realize how long we've waited for...

STEWARDESS. Yeah. Yeah I do Jack. It's RIGHT, God dammit, it's RIGHT. Not one thing in my life is wrong at this moment, truly happy, can you beat that? Happy through all dimensions and backwards and forwards on the calendar happy, Jack, every single cell in me, inside and out, this moment, do you know what I mean? We're in... what are we in... we're in...

JACK. We were always pointed toward this moment, everything we ever —

STEWARDESS. In the event of an emergency, please follow the instructions of the uniformed crew members and be be ready for this. I mean I'm ready for ANYthing. Right? Right. Am I? I am, Jack, I'm ready for anything. I could breathe in the whole world right (*Breathes in deep*) right now, I can do anything with this instant, it's all that matters, we can build the fucking human race from absolutely nothing, Jack, you and me, we can climb

Everest, we can touch the Godhead. We can DO that. YOU HEAR US, WORLD? We... we... we...

JACK. Chart a course for home, Faye, anything.

STEWARDESS. We'd like to thank you. Thank you Jack for making this moment with me. This is as close as people get to feeling what it's like to live forever. We can make this work. We can make anything work. You and me. You hear me?

JACK. (*In awe.*) Yes. I do. I do do do do hear you. (*Little pause.*) Hey look out. (*Sound of screeching tires.*)

STEWARDESS. (*Overlapping on tire sound.*) Jaaaaack it's coming too fast oh CHRIIIIST. (*Pause.*)

JACK. God that was close. Good God, Faye, that was really too — (*Suddenly in overdrive — loudest line of the scene.*) Wrong LANE wrong LANE wrong LANE go back ...

STEWARDESS. (*Faye's last words; she made them count.*) Jack listen to me I love you. (*The sounds of a car crash. Blackout with pinlight spot on Jack, then lights up on Jack and Stewardess.*) Sir?

JACK. Mm?

STEWARDESS. I said we've landed in Boston, sir.

JACK. Oh?

STEWARDESS. Are you all right, sir?

JACK. OH yes. Fine. Not a scratch on me. Nothing on me at all. It was remarkable. (*Pause.*) So I'm supposed to do something. We've landed in...

STEWARDESS. Boston.

JACK. Whatever. Look don't worry about ME. We're on the ground, right? I told you, I'm fine. (*Pause. She begins to move on down the aisle.*) Excuse me, miss. (*She returns to him.*)

STEWARDESS. Yes, sir?

JACK. Nothing. (*She begins to walk away.*)
JACK. Excuse me, miss.
STEWARDESS. Yes, sir?
JACK. Listen. This is entirely inappropriate, and, ah, I have this PowerPoint presentation I'm supposed to give. I'm already late. But all the same, I'd like you to know something.
STEWARDESS. Yes, sir?
JACK. I love you, too. (*She stares at him quizzically, smiles a small smile, walks away. Silence. His cell phone rings. He takes it out of his jacket pocket and stares at it. Slow fade to black as he watches the phone ring.*)

* * *

FANTASIA FAIR

by

Sinan Unel

218 THE BOSTON THEATER MARATHON

Fantasia Fair was produced at the First Annual Boston Theater Marathon on April 18th, 1999. Sponsored by The New African Company. Directed by Ellen Groves. The cast was as follows:
JUDY .... Eleanor Dodd
GEORGE .... Daniel Johns

Fantasia Fair was also produced by the Provincetown Theatre Company as part of the Provincetown Playwrights' Festival on September 25, 1999. It was directed by Sinan Ünel and the cast was as follows.
GEORGE .... John Andert
JUDY .... Susan Grilli

TIME

PLACE
A hotel room. Hotel bed, a chair, bedside table with phone. A dressing table with invisible or real mirror. A door as entry to the room and another door to the bathroom.

FANTASIA FAIR

(*A room in a guesthouse in Provincetown. George and Judy, a couple in their fifties, enter carrying packages.*)

JUDY. Did you hear the phone ring?
GEORGE. No.
JUDY. I thought I heard it from the hallway.
GEORGE. Probably next door.
JUDY. I should call. What if something's wrong?
GEORGE. What could be wrong? You worry too much.
JUDY. Alice had a track meet today and Jennifer had a swimming lesson. I don't know why girls are athletic nowadays. It's so dreadful. What time is it?
GEORGE. We have a few extra minutes. (*Seductively.*) How would her ladyship like to spend them?
JUDY. Off her feet, preferably. Are you going to dress?
GEORGE. Of course.
JUDY. Sorry. Didn't mean to ask the obvious.
GEORGE. It's the highlight of the week. Aren't you excited?
JUDY. Only if you are. I hate trips.
GEORGE. All of them?
JUDY. Yes, honey. I'm always worrying. I'm going to call home.
GEORGE. You talked to them this morning.
JUDY. I don't care. Disasters happen in a matter of

instants.

GEORGE. You just checked the front desk. They would've left a message if something was wrong.

JUDY. Okay, then, I won't call.

GEORGE. Call if you want to.

JUDY. No, you're right. I've become a worry wart hag of some sort.

GEORGE. Will you please call them?

JUDY. No! I refuse. (*George takes out a ballgown, lays it on the bed.*)

JUDY. My goodness. That's really something.

GEORGE. Can I look in your pouch?

JUDY. What pouch?

GEORGE. Your make-up pouch.

JUDY. Oh, sure. What's mine is yours, what's yours is mine. I didn't realize you called it my pouch. Makes me sound like a kangaroo. I call it my bag. My very ordinary, everyday, unglamourous make-up bag. My feet are killing me.

GEORGE. Mine too. That was a long walk.

JUDY. Back and forth, back and forth. The entire town is like a five mile Lord and Taylor. For large women. (*George has started to undress. He'll change completely, to dress as a woman.*)

GEORGE. I'm happy.

JUDY. Sure. You bought a ton of stuff.

GEORGE. I thought you were going to buy that blouse. Did you change your mind?

JUDY. No, I bought it, after all.

GEORGE. Good.

JUDY. (*Takes it out.*) Looked fabulous on the rack but I could tell it was going to look mortally ordinary on me. I've come to realize that most women's clothes look ordinary on most women. They look so glamorous on men. It's the attitude or something. Oh, cherie, or mon amour, I don't know. Men can really do the "wrist" work. If this blouse fit you it would look "fabu," my darling.

GEORGE. I agree. It's a nice blouse.

JUDY. Aren't you going to check the service?

GEORGE. What for?

JUDY. What if there's an emergency? One of your patients or something?

GEORGE. What could I do about that?

JUDY. Your patients depend on you, George. I'm sure it's very frustrating when you're unreachable.

GEORGE. She's going to look gorgeous tonight.

JUDY. They love you, George.

GEORGE. Wanna make love?

JUDY. Now?

GEORGE. Sure. We have a few minutes.

JUDY. You're not listening to me, darling. You're a brilliant doctor. Everyone says so.

GEORGE. I know I am.

JUDY. I mean it, George. Don't underestimate yourself.

GEORGE. Was I just doing that? Why aren't you getting dressed?

JUDY. I am dressed.

GEORGE. This is a ball, Judy. The Fantasia Ball.

JUDY. It's not really a ball. It's a pretend ball.

GEORGE. Yeah, but don't you want to enjoy it?

JUDY. I guess I'll put something on.

GEORGE. (*Sitting on the chair.*) Why don't you come here for a second.

JUDY. Oh, God.

GEORGE. (*Indicating his lap.*) You're upset. Let's talk for a minute.

JUDY. I'm not more upset than usual.

GEORGE. I think you are.

JUDY. I'm just worried about the kids, that's all.

GEORGE. And my emergency calls.

JUDY. I shouldn't come on these things anymore. I'm a nincompoop.

GEORGE. (*Carressing her.*) What would be the point in my coming if you didn't come?

JUDY. Oh, stop. You're always wanting to make love on these things.

GEORGE. We can do it on the bed.

JUDY. I mean these trips. These conventions. And at home when you dress up.

GEORGE. What's wrong with that? I thought you liked it.

JUDY. I'm starting to not like it all that much, George. I'm starting to think there's something kinky about it.

GEORGE. Of course there is. That's the whole goddamn point. Come on. We've been looking forward to this night for a whole year. Let's not do this right now.

JUDY. I have to pick something to wear. What do you think of this?

GEORGE. It's fabu.

JUDY. I can only hope to look as glamorous as you.

GEORGE. As her.

JUDY. Okay. As her. (*Going to the bathroom.*) I wouldn't mind meeting some locals again this year.

GEORGE. That's Thursday night. Mingling with the locals. It's new this year. The convention invites the town to a cocktail party.

JUDY. What do you think of Val and Bill?

GEORGE. You mean Val and Norma Jean.

JUDY. They were Val and Bill at breakfast. I think

FANTASIA FAIR

they want to stay in touch.

GEORGE. That would be fine with me.

JUDY. You never wanted to stay in touch with a couple before.

GEORGE. I'm starting to feel more relaxed.

JUDY. I'll say.

GEORGE. What's that supposed to mean?

JUDY. It means I'll say you're starting to feel more relaxed.

GEORGE. You're really... I'm sorry, you don't want to go to this thing tonight. I shouldn't drag you.

JUDY. I just feel this incremental thing happening, George. This opening up. A widening of some sort. Do you know what happened the other day?

GEORGE. What?

JUDY. Jennifer saw the closet.

GEORGE. She did?

JUDY. Yeah. She was snooping around. Teenagers do that, apparently. And you forgot to lock it. I walked into the room and there she was staring at it, completely aghast.

GEORGE. What did you say?

JUDY. I said they were mine.

GEORGE. Did she believe you?

JUDY. Puhleeze, George. She looked at me like I was a complete idiot and roared with laughter. They hold nothing back, people that age.

GEORGE. Maybe she was amused by your taste in clothes.

JUDY. I should only hope that.

GEORGE. That's alright. I'm going to tell them anyway.

JUDY. Tell them what?

GEORGE. The truth.

JUDY. I hope you won't rush into doing that.

GEORGE. I'm going to tell them when we get back home.

JUDY. You're not serious.

GEORGE. I've been thinking about it for a long time.

JUDY. They're just teenagers, George. They worship you.

GEORGE. Yeah, but they're smart kids. They suspect it anyway.

JUDY. What would be the point, darling? Do you want to shatter their perception of you?

GEORGE. I don't want to hide from them anymore.

JUDY. And then what? Are you going to start dressing around the house, outside of our bedroom? Are you going to come down to dinner like that? Are we going to call you Ginger all the time?

GEORGE. Maybe. Sometimes.

JUDY. Really? Are you going to tell your parents and the people at work? Are you going to drive to the hospital dressed like that and see your patients like that?

GEORGE. I'll probably have my white jacket over my dress.

JUDY. Don't be flip, George, I'm serious. You're scaring me.

GEORGE. I think the kids have a right to know.

JUDY. (*Going to the bathroom.*) I don't think it has anything to do with their rights. You won't tell them right away, George. We have to have a good talk about this first. Maybe see a counselor.

GEORGE. We've seen a counselor already...

JUDY. We'll have to go back to her, George, okay?

GEORGE. Okay. (*Judy goes to the bathroom. She leaves the door open, allowing the light to stream into the*

FANTASIA FAIR 225

room.) This town really does something to me. I get so excited here. These shoes. They're going to look so pretty on her. I can never find shoes Ginger's size anywhere else. Did you see the shoes, Judy?

JUDY. (*Offstage.*) George?

GEORGE. What?

JUDY. (*Offstage.*) Come in here for a minute.

GEORGE. (*Going to the bathroom.*) I hate it when I upset you, baby. The last thing I want is to upset you. I want us to have fun together. (*He sees her through the bathroom door. Stops.*)

JUDY. (*Offstage.*) I'm not upset, darling.

GEORGE. Oh, God. Look at you. You're completely ...

JUDY. (*Offstage.*) ... naked, George. On the bathroom sink. Isn't this the way you wanted me? Come here, George. We've never tried this one before.

GEORGE. (*Goes into the bathroom.*) You're beautiful. You're the best thing that's ever happened to me. You know that? You're everything to me, Judy. My friend, my wife... And you're hot. God, you're so hot right now, darling.

JUDY. (*Offstage.*) Touch my breasts, George. Put your face in them. Bury yourself in them sweetheart. See how real they are?

GEORGE. (*Offstage.*) They're my favorite part of you.

JUDY. (*Offstage.*) Everything about me is real, George. I'm a real woman.

GEORGE. (*Offstage.*) Yes, you are. You're the most real thing I know.

JUDY. (*Suddenly she screams.*) Stop that! (*Comes into the room, putting on her robe.*) I don't like that stuff, don't you understand? How many times have a told you, I don't like that oral stuff like that.

GEORGE. I'm sorry, I got carried away.

JUDY. I thought you weren't going to try to do that again, George.

GEORGE. There's nothing wrong with doing it Judy. People do it all the time.

JUDY. There's nothing wrong with anything, George. Where does it stop?

GEORGE. You're being silly, now, you're making this a huge big...

JUDY. I'm not that person in there, George. Getting naked, perching on a bathroom sink cooing like a moronic pigeon. I don't know who that is but it would not be me.

GEORGE. Then why?

JUDY. I'm not the person who goes to these functions with you and acts like she's your girlfriend or your sister and calls you Ginger and acts like you're a real woman in front of all those strangers. Ginger did this, Ginger did that, she bought those fabulous shoes and we're the best of friends, all that crap. I'm not that person, don't you see? I don't know who I am anymore. Nothing about me is real. I'm not real, George. I don't know who I am. Don't tell the children, please. I'm begging you. It's the last thing I can bear. Don't make me pretend in front of my own children too. (*George puts on his wig.*)

GEORGE. When I was a little girl, Judy...

JUDY. You were never a little girl, my darling. You were a little boy.

GEORGE. When I was, Judy... Please, Judy.

JUDY. I want to know who I'm with.

GEORGE. When I was a little girl, I had a visitor at nights. She was an aunt, I think, or somebody like that. At night she'd come to my room. She was large. Her breasts were large and her arms were soft and all encompassing, just ... wide all over. She'd sweat all the time, just lightly and sweetly and was always moist and warm. She smelled of lilacs and her voice was more resonant than a violin and more beautiful. She always wore beautiful clothes. She dripped of honey and she loved everyone and forgave everything. That's how she was to me. She was the mother of all sins and all sinners and all the bad children and she forgave them all. There's a woman living secretly in all of us that bears our secret origins. I don't think you believe me, Judy, but when I was a little girl, she visited me at night.

JUDY. I believe you.

GEORGE. Some nights she'd stay with me til dawn and teach me how to dress. Let your hands do it, my baby, she'd say. It's like music. Let your hands play the music. (*The phone rings. Judy answers it.*)

JUDY. Hello? Oh, hi, darling. I was worrying about you. How did the swim go. Well, I'm sorry about that dear, but there will be other ones. We're fine. I'm sitting here relaxing, reading a book. You're father's at a meeting. I hardly see him, these medical conventions are so dreadful, I'm not going to come to them anymore. I'm glad you called, dear. Call every night, okay? And I'll see you Monday when we get home. I miss you Jenny, and I love you dear. Bye. (*She hangs up. George is dressed and ready.*)

GEORGE. I don't know what I'd do without you. You're more precious to me than anything in the world. But if you want to go, Judy, take the next flight out...

JUDY. I'm here now, Ginger. It's okay.

GEORGE. I told the girls I'd meet them for a cocktail before dinner. Come down and join us as soon as you're dressed.

JUDY. Okay. (*They kiss. He exits. Judy looks at*

herself in the mirror. Places a wig on her head.) I'm already dressed, you moron. (*Smiles. Strikes a pose.*) I'm dressed for the ball. (*Fade to black.*)

* * *

ROOM 69

by

Bruce Ward

Room 69 premiered at the First Annual Boston Theater Marathon on April 18th, 1999. Sponsored by The Coyote Theatre. Directed by Courtney Oconnor. The cast was as follows:

HAL .... John Porell
STEVE .... Chip Phillips
ELEANOR .... Dorothy Dwyer
DORIS .... Cheryl McMahon

CHARACTERS

STEVE — Casually Conservative, Early to Late 30's
HAL — Conventionally Conservative, Early to Late 30's
DORIS — Assertive, Aggressive, Confident, 30's to 40's
ELEANOR — meek, "mousy", confused, late 20's to Early 30's

TIME
Early evening.

PLACE
A classroom.

ROOM 69

(*A classroom with a blackboard, several chairs. A pair of dress shoes and khaki pants are all we see of Hal, who is hidden behind the blackboard. He is writing something on the back side of the board. He stops, erases. Writes something else. Stops, reads what he has written. Steve enters. He is mid-30s, attractive, dressed casually, but neatly. He enters, silent and a bit nervous, looks around, walks in. Hal peers around the blackboard. He is also mid-to-late thirties, dressed conservatively in buttoned-down shirt and slacks.*)

HAL. Hello.
STEVE. Oh Jesus...! I mean my God... I mean... gosh ...
HAL. Sorry.
STEVE. You startled me.
HAL. I'm sorry.
STEVE. I was... (*He stops, stares at Hal.*) You!
HAL. Um... sorry... ?
STEVE. What are you... ?
HAL. I'm sorry, I don't...
STEVE. Oh that is great, that really is. Wait a minute, wait a minute, is this... (*Taking out a piece of paper.*) Room 69? This is Room 69, isn't it?

HAL. Uh, yes. I believe so. I mean I really don't...
STEVE. I'd better go.
HAL. What? Wait. No, please. You've got the right ... I mean, you are here for the... you're here for the meeting, right?
STEVE. (*Cautiously.*) Which meeting?
HAL. You're here for the meeting, I know. I can tell.
STEVE. What do you mean you can tell? You can't tell. How can you tell?
HAL. Calm down, that's not what I...
STEVE. You don't remember me, do you? That's rich. That's just rich. Here we are, at this meeting, you're the... what? The g.d. facilitator or something? Do you work here? Do you run this thing?
HAL. Well I don't... I don't run it, no, but yes, I facilitate several meetings, including this one. And no, I'm sorry, I don't remember you. Should I? I'm sorry.
STEVEN. Never mind.
HAL. Look, the others will be here very shortly. Maybe you should tell me what this is about. (*Steve looks nervous. Hal leads him to a chair. They both sit.*)
HAL. Look, I know there are several things in all of our pasts... in everyone's past who comes here, to this meeting, but.. well, that's why we're here, isn't it? To get beyond that, to move on, to deal with, yes, even to accept those... distortions... in our past, to acknowledge and to accept. And to change. The past. To recover. To reclaim the values and morals in which we truly believe.
STEVE. The bushes.
HAL. What... I'm sorry...
STEVE. (*In a tense whisper.*) The bushes. The bushes. In the goddman... the g.d. bushes.
HAL. The bu... what bushes? What are you talking

about?

STEVE. The bushes! You know what bushes I'm talking about! And don't stand there and tell me you don't know who the hell... the heck I am. And stop staring at my butt.

HAL. Wha... You have gone... you are going a bit too far there, mister.

STEVE. I saw it! I saw it.

HAL. (*A tense whisper.*) Now listen! They will be here any minute. Don't you understand what I'm talking about? That is why we're here...

STEVE. Then you admit it.

HAL. Admit what?

STEVE. The bushes. The bushes down across the plaza. You've been there.

HAL. Listen, that doesn't matter now.

STEVE. Fine. It doesn't matter now. But you've been there.

HAL. So what if I've been there, that's all in the...

STEVE. Past, yeah, I got it But you remember me.

HAL. Look, I may have been there one or two times, temptation overcame me, I was weak, I was wrong, I sinned, I admit it, but nothing ever happened.

STEVE. Nothing ever... You call that nothing?

HAL. I wish you'd calm down, they'll be here...

STEVE. It wasn't even any good.

HAL. Wha... How dare you? That is an evil thing to say little missy.

STEVE. Then you remember?

HAL. I don't know what in Jesus' name you're talking about, but if it's what I think you're talking about, I can assure you, you don't know what you're talking about. There was no problem in that arena, fella.

STEVE. That's not how I recall it. On several occasions. Once or twice!?

HAL. Are you questioning my virility? You... you faggy little pansy.

STEVE. You take that back!

HAL. I will not.

STEVE. You take that back or I will tell everyone in this room that not only are you queer, but you're a bad queer at that!

HAL. (*Becoming "hissy".*) You are a pathetic little homosexual person. To think that I would even cast a glance at someone as hopelessly bland as you, no wonder I couldn't get it up. And don't flatter yourself, you've got a flat ass.

STEVE. I do not! I am always complimented for my rear end. Women. Women always remark. I can hear them. Behind my back. And sometimes in front of it, too.

HAL. Who's complimenting you, Linda Tripp?

STEVE. You leave her out of this! She's looking pretty good now. (*Doris enters, wearing slacks, flannel shirt, carrying a briefcase.*)

DORIS. Sorry I'm late, some fucking idiot tried to take the parking spot I was waiting for for ten minutes. Can you believe the frigging nerve of the asshole? And then he tries to block me from getting in the spot, and I'm three and a half minutes late and you know how I hate that. Well obviously he had no idea who he was dealing with, and I get out the car, and he gets out of the car, and he's a little bald guy with his hair combed over his head, and one of those stupid hairy things that make him look like a goat, and he starts to open his mouth and I just give him one of my famous stares... (*She does.*) and he stands there like this... (*She imitates him, jaw wide open.*) and he just backs away and gets into his Ford Explorer and I'm still standing there... (*She goes back to her stare.*) and he drives away, still looking at me the whole way... (*She looks sheepishly.*) I can even see him looking in the rear-view mirror. Hah! Never even said a goddamned word! How's them apples? (*To Steve.*) Oh, you must be new. Doris. Welcome. (*To Hal.*) Is this it? Where is everyone? (*To Steve.*) What's your name?

STEVE. Uh, Steve.

DORIS. Where the hell is everyone?

HAL. I don't know. Maybe late. I know Binky had a PTA meeting.

DORIS. Goddman PTA. Always a problem. Binky. What kind of a hell of a name is Binky for a grown woman? Jesus, five last week, now two and one of them new. (*To Steve.*) Well, you look good, you'll be good in front of cameras. You ever do interviews? Do you speak? Let's hear you. Speak. Say something.

STEVE. Uh...

DORIS. Never mind, we'll train you. Just keep yourself well-groomed. Are you married yet?

STEVE. Well, no...

DORIS. Never mind, we'll find you a girlfriend. Hal here's got a couple. (*To Hal.*) How's your... what's her name, Sarah, Sally, the one with the perky tits.

HAL. Susan. She's fine.

DORIS. You done it yet? Never mind, none of my business. But you gotta do it, that's important. Damn, I'd like to see that.

HAL. What?

DORIS. She's a perky one, that one. Nice skin. Good taste in clothes. What's that scent she uses, again? She told me...

HAL. I don't remember, listen I think we have a problem here...

DORIS. Well, never mind. So it's the three of us. Fuck 'em. Fuck 'em all. We'll do it ourselves, we don't have much time, they'll be here soon, we've got to re-cap for the big kahuna. (*To Steve.*) You know what that is, kid?

STEVE. What's that?

DORIS. The big kahuna.

STEVE. Is this a trick question?

DORIS. We're meeting with that gay group from, where is it Hal?

STEVE. Medford...

DORIS. Medford! Can you believe it? A goddamn gay group in Medford! We're meeting next door with them and the neighborhood council in less than half an hour. We've got to show them our stuff, reclaim our people.

STEVE. Uh, right on.

DORIS. (*Going to blackboard.*) Okay, let's talk strategy. Quickly. (*She flips over blackboard — or turns it around. On it, Hal has written Welcome to Recovering Homosexuals, You're At Home Now. She draws diagrams on the board as she speaks.*) Tonight we are facing the enemy. This is what the enemy looks like. (*She takes out magazine cut-out pictures of Richard Simmons, Ellen DeGeneres, and Liberace and places them on the board with tape that has been pre-affixed.*) This is us. (*She places cut-outs of Arnold Schwartznegger, Bruce Willis and Elizabeth Dole on the opposite side of the blackboard.*) Tonight we meet with them at the Medford town meeting, where the enemy will attempt to manipulate with lies, innuendo and bitchy sarcasm. They will attempt to penetrate our spiritual beliefs with filthy bon-mots and facetious wit. And they will, no doubt, have an array of delectable hors d'oeuvres with which to tempt the hungry masses. But we! We will counter-attack. Little do they know we have provided our own culinary surprise. (*She goes to the door.*) Eleanor, you may come in now! (*To the men.*) Our secret weapon. Our own Eleanor Magnabox, caterer to the rich and famous pediatricians, obstetricians, and orthodontists of Brookline, Sudbury and Beacon Hill. (*Eleanor enters, meek and mousy.*)

ELEANOR. (*With trays of food in hand.*) Should I just ... ?

DORIS. That's fine, El. Thank you. It looks lovely. (*Eleanor deposits trays of food, stands there, uncertain.*) Uh, gentlemen, this is Eleanor. My roommate. Eleanor, Hal, and, uh...

STEVE. Steve.

DORIS. Steve. Unfortunately, Eleanor has to go now, don't you, Eleanor?

ELEANOR. Doris.

DORIS. El.

ELEANOR. DORIS!

DORIS. EL! (*Eleanor starts to cry.*) O-KAY!

ELEANOR. I never see you anymore...

DORIS. We're in the middle of a meeting here, El...

STEVE. What seems to be the... Is there something I can...

HAL. Stay out of it, you've already created enough...

DORIS. Oh for God's sake. El, have a seat. We're almost through here. We need to proceed, the meeting is in fifteen minutes. (*Steve takes Eleanor by the arm, leads her to a chair, helps her sit.*)

STEVE. Are you all right?

ELEANOR. Yes. Yes, I'm sorry. I'm very sorry. It's just that... I thought that we... She said that she... and now she's... I'm so confused... (*She starts to cry again.*)

DORIS. (*Taking up where she left off.*) At stake: a proposal by the enemy to establish a domestic partners benefits program in the city of Medford, a proposal which would mean... (*She places the photo of Liberace next to the photo of Richard Simmons.*)... or even... (*She places the photo of Ellen DeGeneres next to the photo of Eleanor Dole.*)... which we all know could lead to this... (*She pulls out a paper cut-out of a group of children, places it on the bottom of the board, pulls out a "Tinky Winky" teletubby doll from her bag, and "attacks" the children with Tinky Winky.*) The implications are clear. Our children's lives are at stake. (*Eleanor raises her hand.*) What is it, Eleanor?

ELEANOR. But we don't have any children.

DORIS. I'm speaking metaphorically, darli... Eleanor. I'm speaking of all our children. And of our future children.

ELEANOR. I thought you didn't want children.

DORIS. El, if you cannot participate here, you can leave. (*Eleanor starts to cry. Steve puts her arm around her.*) DON'T TOUCH HER!

STEVE. Don't yell at her.

HAL. Why don't you stay out of it?

STEVE. Why don't you go back to the bushes where you belong?

HAL. (*Very tense, sotto voce.*) Will you...

DORIS. What was that?

HAL. Nothing! Shut up.

ELEANOR. Don't pick on her.

DORIS. (*To Steve.*) Wait a minute, ARE YOU AN INFILTRATOR?!

ELEANOR. Don't pick on him.

DORIS. ELEANOR, BE QUIET!

STEVE. Don't yell at her! (*Eleanor starts to cry.*)

HAL. (*Going to Eleanor.*) See what you've made her do?

STEVE. See what *I've* made her do? You're the one who made her cry! (*They are each tugging at Eleanor.*)

HAL. No, *you're* the one who made her cry.

STEVE. No, *you!*

HAL. No, *you!*

DORIS. DON'T TOUCH HER!

ELEANOR. Stop yelling! (*She inadvertently grabs Hal's hair, pulls off his toupee... or possibly, a "clip-on" tie, Hal gasps in horror, Steve bursts out laughing.*)

DORIS. (*Looks out window.*) Oh my God, they're on their way... we have to get ready. Pull yourselves together, for God's sake. (*She goes behind blackboard, where there are signs on posts that read "God created Adam and Eve, not Adam and Steve" and "Bert and Ernie Are Just Roommates".*)

STEVE. No, I am not an infiltrator. I came to this meeting because... because I thought I believed it. I wanted to believe it.

DORIS. Shut up and take a sign. You too, Eleanor.

STEVE. I thought... if I could change... if it were true, if I could lead a normal life, a life that society says is normal, things would be easier... But you people are crazy!

ELEANOR. (*Reading sign that says "Hey Hey What Do You Say, You Don't Have To Be That Way".*) I don't understand...

DORIS. Come on, they're coming!

STEVE. I'm not coming.

ELEANOR. I'm not coming, either!

DORIS. Eleanor!

ELEANOR. (*Firm and proud.*) I'm taking Max, and moving to my sister's.

DORIS. Eleanor Magnabox, I forbid you to take that Doberman!

ELEANOR. You forbid? Poof! Be gone! You have no power here.

STEVE. You tell her, Glinda.

HAL. (*Straightening his toupee.*) Screw them both, let's go, I'm sure the others are down there already.

DORIS. (*Hesitates for a moment, then to Eleanor.*) I'll deal with you later. (*Squaring off, to Steve.*) It comes to no good when a stranger in our midst starts to stir things up.

STEVE. (*Matching her in stance, a la Gary Cooper.*) I'll remember that at high noon tomorrow.

DORIS. (*Gives Steve a dirty look, then, to Hal.*) Let's go.

HAL. (*To Steve.*) You... You... Tinkerbell! (*Doris and Hal leave.*)

STEVE. (*Calling after him.*) Sticks and stones may break my bones... besides, I love Tinkerbell! (*After a moment's pause.*) And Tinky-Winky too! (*He looks towards Eleanor. A moment of silence. Then, to her...*) Well.

ELEANOR. Well.

STEVE. How about a cup of coffee? (*Eleanor hesitates a moment, then smiles, holds out her arm. Steve takes it, they begin to exit.*)

ELEANOR. Wait! (*She runs to her tray of food, picks it up.*) They forgot their secret weapon. Let's pig out! (*They laugh, walk off arm in arm. Lights fade.*)

* * *

www.ingramcontent.com/pod-product-compliance
Lightning Source LLC
Chambersburg PA
CBHW052017290426
44112CB00014B/2279